DATE DUE

MY 29 97			
SE 16 97			
MR 6 98			
JA 20 98			
DE 3 98			
AP 6 99			
MY 4 99			
OC 12 99			
JA 24 00			
DE 19 01			
DE 18 03			
AP 7 04			

THE
BEST
AMERICAN
SHORT
PLAYS
1995-1996

Best American Short Plays Series

THE
BEST
AMERICAN
SHORT
PLAYS
1995-1996

edited by

HOWARD STEIN
and
GLENN YOUNG

THE BEST AMERICAN SHORT PLAYS 1995-1996

Copyright ©1997 by Applause Theatre Book Publishers
All Rights Reserved
ISBN 1-55783-254-4 (cloth), 1-55783-255-2 (paper)
ISSN 0067-6284

Applause Theatre Book Publishers   **A&C Black**

211 West 71st Street   Howard Road, Eaton Socon
New York, NY 10023   Huntingdon, Cambs PC19 3CZ
Phone: (212) 595-4735   Phone: 01480-212666
Fax: (212) 721-2856   Fax: 01480-405014

First Applause Printing, 1997

CONTENTS

To Marianne and Priscilla

INTRODUCTION

Home and the family have been major subjects for the American playwright for the better part of this century. Ben Brantley, daily theater critic for *The New York Times*, defines a bona fide classic family play as "a work that conveys the mystical, cannibalistic pull of family ties even as they unravel." This description aptly sums up Brantley's reaction to *Buried Child* by Sam Shepard, and could as well fit Eugene O'Neill's *Long Day's Journey Into Night*. However, it is less appropriate a description for the family plays that overran Broadway and the American theater from 1920 to 1960, which include *They Knew What They Wanted, The Little Foxes, Awake and Sing, Holiday, All My Sons, Death of a Salesman, Glass Menagerie, Cat On A Hot Tin Roof, Dark At The Top Of The Stairs, Picnic,* and finally, in 1959, *A Raisin In The Sun*. Nevertheless, these plays and their concentration on the American Family gave energy, muscle, and stamina to the development of the nation's theater. Indeed, the entire culture was always alluding to Home and the Family through songs and novels, as well as through plays: "Home Is Where The Heart Is"; "Show Me The Way To Go Home"; "Home, Home On The Range"; "You Can't Go Home Again"; *The Long Voyage Home*; and finally *Home*, by Samm-Art Williams.

The theater reflected and illuminated society's preoccupation. But where classical plays such as *The Oresteia* used the family to dramatize the subject of Justice, where *Hamlet* and *King Lear* used the family to dramatize the scope of the human spirit, and where Molière's comedies used the family to dramatize "Lord, what fools we mortals be," American plays used the family to present familiar situations and problems that pervaded American society. Conflicts between parents and children, husbands and wives, and sisters and brothers brought to light family dilemmas that cut across social, economic, and psychological barriers, revealing and representing what was close to "home" in the American family. The American family was thus both glorified and unmasked.

With a few significant exceptions (Lanford Wilson, Neil Simon, and A. R. Gurney), American family drama was forever changed with the 1960 production of Edward Albee's *The American Dream*. This short play exploded the myth of the American family, causing the subject of Home to be treated in an entirely new fashion. Kopit's *Oh,Dad, Poor Dad, etc.* and David Rabe's *Sticks and Bones*, plays that appeared in New York City within a few years of Albee's, were satiric in tone, surreal in treatment, and severe in their attitude toward family life. Nevertheless, fascination with the topic of Family has continued, even if, perhaps, with less intensity. For example, in the summer of 1995, the Mc-Carter Theater in Princeton organized a series of short plays for Random Acts, their new-works festival, under the guidance of Emily Mann, Artistic Director, and Janice Paran, Dramaturg and Supervisor. Paran assigned the subject "Home" to the playwrights, all of whom were commissioned to write for the festival. Two of those plays are included in this volume: *Home Section*, by Janusz Glowacki and *The Sandalwood Box*, by Mac Wellman.

Since the 1960s, however, interest has shifted from the American family to America itself. Inspired by the Vietnam War and the Civil Rights Movement, playwrights inundated the theater with plays dealing with the past, present, and future of America. Listen to the titles: *America Hurrah, God Bless, 1776, 1492, Indians, U.S., We Bombed In New Haven, Blues For Mister Charlie, Viet Rock, MacBird*... the list goes on. Playwrights today continue to explore the nation as a whole, rather than the individual families that comprise it. In this year's volume of *The Best American Short Plays*, we have included a comic narrative in one act called *The Original Last Wish Baby*, by William Seebring, which attacks American culture, values, and attitudes. One scene ridicules the conventional talk show by having a pundit say, "The phenomenon speaks directly to who we are as a nation." Although the line is written in a mocking tone, the content is all too familiar.

Cassandra Medley's *Dearborn Heights* is a very different play from Seebring's satire. Copyrighted in 1995, the drama takes place in Michigan in 1951, and deals with the hypocritical, damaging, and humiliating treatment of American blacks by American whites. Medley then takes the story one step further to show how that abuse can tear the black community apart by causing American blacks to turn on each other. The subject is especially appropriate for 1996 America. Jonathan Levy's *Old Blues* also harks back to another time, the time of the old college try and old college ties and the romanticism of college singing groups. But, like *Dearborn Heights*, this play is haunted by an off-stage presence. In *Dearborn Heights* that presence is the unseen white customers in the cafe, whose stares and glares grow into an ominous, smothering cloud of disapproval. In *Old Blues*, the dead companion, who has died with his boots on as a charter member of the group, represents the values of the anachronistic nature of the group he left behind. The plays indirectly direct themselves to present-day America.

Lavonne Mueller, in her *American Dreamers*, writes about a fictional encounter in 1962 during which Carl Sandburg joins forces with Marilyn Monroe to consider the present and future of America and its dreams. Mueller's imaginative and inventive rendering of two American icons meeting under extraordinary conditions (she used a similar device in *Little Victories*, where Susan B. Anthony joins forces with Joan of Arc) allows her to express, through them, her concern for this nation. Michael Feingold, on the other hand, uses the playwrighting techniques of the past to shed light not only on the conventions of nineteenth-century playmaking, but also on the narrow minds of the twentieth-century playgoer. Feingold does not confine his sharp bites to America, by any means.

Perhaps the most telling subject among the plays in this volume is that of faith, the nation's most critical and crucial issue, especially faith in love. Paul Selig's *Mystery School* portrays three women struggling with belief as a source of immediate, as well as eternal, salvation; as a means of dealing with both the present and the future. Allan Knee's *The St. Valentine's Day Massacre* would appear to be a conventional drama of two lovers, or ex-lovers, in a "same time next year" ritual. But, in the course of their exchange, Kenny recognizes unbearable signs in Sherry—as he says with a note of alarm, "I get the feeling you don't believe in love anymore, either." While teaching at Columbia, I met one day with our master teacher of Directing, Liviu Ciulei, who startled me by announcing that he had confronted his students that very morning and concluded that they didn't believe in love. I tried, unsuccessfully, to calm him down. Later that day, I called our youngest son, Josh, age 36, and asked him if he thought his generation believed in love. His answer was, "My generation, Dad, can't afford love. They can afford big cars, long trips, international vacations, state of the art stereo equipment, but they can't afford love."

Monroe, in *American Dreamers*, claims that with her devotion and passion for the President, "This love is going to save the world." Not the lovers, not the community, not the nation, not the hemisphere, but the world. Ed, in *Degas, C'est Moi*, calls out, "…are Edgar Degas and I not united by our shared humanity? By our common need for love?" *Fitting Rooms* opens with a conversation between two female friends of long standing, about marriage and happiness, the central issue being the changing nature of love. Their faith in what love can accomplish has eroded to the point of collapse. But, by the end of the play, it is clear that for these two women, and for the others in the fitting rooms next to them, the only fitting room, the ultimate fitting room, is love. While *Degas, C'est Moi*, and *St. Valentine's Day Massacre* both deal with youthful love, John Ford Noonan's *When It Comes Early* deals with aging love. Although the play has flashes of the vigor and vitality of the couple's early love, the bulk of the story concentrates on the human, generous, and compassionate nature of their aging love, as both life and love begin to disintegrate before their eyes. The scope is considerable, but the message is clear: love may not conquer all, but we are nothing without it.

> Of all the things America has lost
> It's faith in love it misses most.

When this volume appears in bookstores, I will be approaching my seveny-fifth birthday. Time to stop and concentrate on my wife, my children, and my grandchildren...maybe golf. I am especially grateful to Glenn Young for having given me the opportunity to co-edit with him the last six volumes, and I wish *The Best American Short Plays,* under his discerning stewardship, a long and fruitful life. And to you, the readers, at the risk of sounding like Kate Smith, thanks for listening.

Howard Stein
September, 1996

Susan Cinoman

FITTING ROOMS

SUSAN CINOMAN

Fitting Rooms was first seen at the Ensemble Studio Theatre, and later at Naked Angels under the direction of Jane Hoffman. Other plays by Susan Cinoman, including *Sweet Sand, Temple Beautiful,* and *Gin and Bitters,* were also presented at EST. A full production of one-acts titled *Cinoman and Rebeck,* were presented by the Miranda Theatre Company at Alice's Fourth Floor in New York City and received critical acclaim.

Susan Cinoman began as an actress and sketch comedy writer in Philadelphia with her all-female comedy group, "The Soubrettes," with whom she recorded the song "Bimbo Rap." She has gone on to be included in the Maxwell Anderson Playwrights Series at the Rich Forum in Stamford, Connecticut, and is an active member of the Miranda Theatre Company and the Theatre Artists Workshop of Westport. Her first musical, *Out of the Blues,* which she wrote with composer Joe Goodrich, is currently being produced by the Miranda Theatre Company. Her latest full length play, *Love and Class in Connecticut,* is forthcoming. Cinoman lives in the aforementioned Connecticut with her husband and her two daughters.

SETTING: *A tony boutique on Philadelphia's Rittenhouse Square. The clothing is elegant and chic with a few bizarre and hideous originals that are there to appeal to some of the clientele. The three pairs of women change clothes in three separate fitting rooms. The action switches quickly from one dressing room to another.*

MARIEL: My husband would kill me if I bought this dress.

LINDA: You're kidding.

MARIEL: Well, no. I mean, I don't think he would literally kill me. But I know he wouldn't be very happy.

LINDA: Well, who cares about that.

MARIEL: That's true.

LINDA: I mean it's not as if he makes you happy.

MARIEL: But can anyone really make anyone else happy?

LINDA: What do you mean?

MARIEL: I mean don't you have to make yourself happy.

LINDA: I guess that's true. All the more reason for you to buy the dress.

MARIEL: You don't care what any man thinks about you, do you?

LINDA: No.

MARIEL: How do you manage that?

LINDA: I think about other things.

MARIEL: Like what?

LINDA: Like your marriage. Pamela's marriage. All your marriages.

MARIEL: But how does that do it for you?

LINDA: I don't know really. Between that and work I'm busy.

[*Light change to* RISSA *and* KATE.]

RISSA: Did you want to try that on, Mrs. Oliver?

KATE: Yes. Thank you, Rissa.

RISSA: That's a good color for you.

KATE: It is?

RISSA: Definitely.

KATE: How can you tell?

RISSA: How can I tell?

KATE: Yes. How do you know?

RISSA: You're a Winter.

KATE: What am I?

RISSA: A Winter. I'm a Summer. My most beautiful colors are red and yellow. Now that color would look good on me, but not great. It would make the green tones in my skin come out. But, if I wanted to look beautiful I wouldn't wear that color, but you would. Because you're cold. Very cold.

KATE: Do you have this dress in red or yellow?

RISSA: Yes. But, you won't look as beautiful in it. Remember? Cold. Winter?

KATE: Yes, that's right.

RISSA: Sure.

KATE: Then I guess I'll try this on. In this color.

RISSA: That seems to be the way to go.

KATE: Uh-huh.

RISSA: This is going very well.

KATE: Mmm.

RISSA: For you.

[*Light change to* MARIEL *and* LINDA.]

MARIEL: I think I look like an eel in this.

LINDA: I love it on you.

MARIEL: I don't think Gary will.

LINDA: Gary.

MARIEL: He is my husband.

LINDA: But not your father.

MARIEL: But he'll say it's too tight.

LINDA: So? What will he do? Ground you?

MARIEL: It's easy for you to say.

LINDA: Yes. It is.

MARIEL: I'm just trying to do the right thing.

LINDA: It's not a moral issue. It's just rayon.

MARIEL: I mean I'm trying to be a good partner.

LINDA: But it's your wardrobe.

MARIEL: But I'm his wife.

LINDA: But it's your body.

MARIEL: But it's his charge card.

LINDA: But it's your signature.

MARIEL: It's so hard to know what to wear.

LINDA: Look, wearing clothes is just like anything else. It seems really important to you how you look. But, basically after the first minute that someone sees you they pay no attention, anyway. So, you might as well do what you want to do.

MARIEL: That doesn't make me feel better.

LINDA: Is that my function? Am I here to make you feel better?

MARIEL: As my friend, yes.

LINDA: Is that what friends are for?

MARIEL: Among other things.

LINDA: You never make me feel better.

MARIEL: But that's not within my power.

LINDA: But it's in mine for you.

MARIEL: Yes.

LINDA: And why is that?

MARIEL: Because you're the independent one.

LINDA: So?

MARIEL: So, I'm the dependent one.

LINDA: OK...

MARIEL: And the dependent one can't make the independent one feel better.

LINDA: Then what can the dependent one do for the independent one?

MARIEL: You mean after the independent one makes the dependent one feel better?

LINDA: Yes. What does the independent one get to feel?

MARIEL: Superior.

LINDA: I see.

MARIEL: But not better. Only the independent one has the power there.

LINDA: So, if I make you feel better and persuade you that you don't look like an eel, then I get to feel superior.

MARIEL: Yes.

LINDA: You don't look like an eel.

MARIEL: Really?

LINDA: Absolutely.

MARIEL: Now, I feel better. Will you ask the salesgirl if they have this a size smaller?

[KAHINE *and* TIA *enter. They are very young and thin, dressed in tight tops and denim skirts or jeans with lots of black touches, maybe all black, red lipstick.*]

KAHINE: Where are the prom dresses?

TIA: Oh cool, Ka. Look at this one.

KAHINE: That's more your type of thing.

TIA: But . . . it goes with your hair.

KAHINE: My hair's gonna be burgundy, I told you that.

TIA: Well, I forgot. Like, have me arrested or something. Is Suzanne Vega gay?

KAHINE: Probably.

TIA: All the cool people seem to be gay. Don't you think?

KAHINE: Cool boots.

TIA: They're not very retro.

KAHINE: So?

TIA: So . . . I thought that was what you liked.

KAHINE: Retro is going out.

TIA: You're kidding?

KAHINE: I'm dead serious.

TIA: Wow.

KAHINE: What's coming in is Eco. Like, plants and animals.

TIA: Really?

KAHINE: Yeah. All different species. They say it's because of the Berlin Wall.

TIA: What Berlin Wall?

KAHINE: You know, the one that fell.

TIA: Are the Berlin Wall and The Iron Curtain the same thing?

KAHINE: Tia, one's a wall and one's a curtain.

TIA: Oh.

KAHINE: They can't be the same thing.

TIA: So, where are we having the prom? Did the commitee decide it?

KAHINE: Tatou.

TIA: Cool.

KAHINE: Of course, Danielle didn't even know where it was.

TIA: Danielle is an asshole.

KAHINE: Please. Who isn't?

TIA: You. You're not.

KAHINE: Well.

TIA: Am I?

KAHINE: No. You're not. But you will be if you try that scanky thing on.

[*Change to* LINDA *and* MARIEL.]

LINDA: I don't see the sales girl.

MARIEL: Do you like the back of this?

LINDA: Yes. I told you to buy it.

MARIEL: Don't get hostile, please.

LINDA: Mariel, I'd like to go have lunch.

MARIEL: You sound just like Gary.

LINDA: No, I don't.

MARIEL: You do. He doesn't understand that it takes me time to make a decision. He doesn't understand that I get anxiety when I'm rushed. He likes me to feel anxiety.

LINDA: I don't like you to feel anxiety.

MARIEL: You must because you're rushing me.

LINDA: I'm sorry.

MARIEL: I told you that it might take some time to find the right dress.

LINDA: I know.

MARIEL: I told you that I'd wait for you to finish work so I didn't feel rushed.

LINDA: You're right.

MARIEL: And then you rush me anyway.

LINDA: You're right. I'm sorry.

MARIEL: You are?

LINDA: I'm deeply sorry.

MARIEL: You're my best friend.

LINDA: I know.

MARIEL: You're the only one I can talk to.

LINDA: I know.

MARIEL: If it wasn't for you I'd just stay at home and wait for Gary.

LINDA: I know. I know.

MARIEL: It's no picnic having a rich husband, you know.

LINDA: I'm sure it's very difficult for you.

MARIEL: You don't really think it's difficult.

LINDA: Sure, I do.

MARIEL: No, you don't. You don't know what it's like to have to be enthusiastic over someone else's accomplishments all day long.

LINDA: No...

MARIEL: And to have to be the perennial hostess, and to have to sexually service someone even when you don't feel like it just to know that you can have breakfast the next morning.

LINDA: Jesus, Mariel...

MARIEL: Well, it's true.

LINDA: Then why do it?

MARIEL: Do what?

LINDA: Why be a well paid minion if it makes you so miserable?

MARIEL: Well... because...

LINDA: Yes?

MARIEL: Because what's the alternative?

LINDA: The alternative...

MARIEL: Isn't the alternative... to be you?

[*Change to* RISSA *and* KATE.]

RISSA: I think I like this one better.

KATE: I... I appreciate all your time, Rissa...

RISSA: No problem. I mean you're welcome, Mrs. Oliver. You know, I hate when people say thank you, and people say back to them, "No problem." Like, you didn't say, "Is this a problem," to which I would answer, "No problem." You said, "I appreciate that," to which I answer, "you're welcome." You know what I mean?

KATE: I do.

RISSA: I know. You know a lot of that I picked up from you, Mrs. Oliver.

KATE: What?

RISSA: You know, the right way to be. You come in, you look nice, you talk enough, but not too loud. In my neighborhood everybody screams. And the grammar. I mean you could break your neck tripping over the G's that get dropped all up and down Ninth Street. Not that I inspire to be an intellectual snob. But someday I'd like to own this business. Someday I'll be finished at Drexel...I...are you OK, Mrs. Oliver?

KATE: Actually I'm having a little trouble with the zipper.

RISSA: Here...let me...

KATE: Oh, thank you...I appreciate that...

RISSA: Now, wait...see, this is an Osaki...see, this is a challenge here...it's a tiny little thing here in the zipper, like something that they use in lasers. You know the Japanese.

KATE: Yes.

RISSA: Fusing fashion and high tech. You know how they do that.

KATE: Well, thank you.

RISSA: No problem.

KATE: What do you think?

RISSA: It's a great winter color for you.

KATE: Really?

RISSA: Rich, but not overly rich. Youthful. Perfect. What exactly were you looking for?

KATE: A dress to meet my daughter in.

RISSA: What? You never met your daughter before?

KATE: Oh...I...

RISSA: Mrs. Oliver? Are you OK?

KATE: I'm sorry.

RISSA: Don't be sorry. You just went a little white there. Maybe you'd want to be trying this stuff on by yourself.

KATE: No, that's all right, I...

RISSA: I'm just picking something up here. I'm very funny that way. About people. And their feelings.

KATE: I'm a little nervous these days.

RISSA: You know, I thought that on Thursday. When you came in Thursday.

KATE: What?

RISSA: I thought, Mrs.Oliver seems nervous today. Or, not nervous exactly . . . uptight.

KATE: Really?

RISSA: I swear to God. I made a mental note of it.

KATE: About me?

RISSA: Well, you're my customer, Mrs. Oliver. And, I mean, you know, I read about you in the paper all the time, and your benefits that you give and all, and you always come back in here. It's very important to us. To me. It's important, and not just because of money.

KATE: No?

RISSA: Well . . . it's because of money, because it would be good to have money, and so someone is naturally interested in money, but, for me . . . it's you. Because of your . . . carriage.

KATE: I don't know.

RISSA: It's just, I admire that in you. Because, me, in my field, the fashion field, you know, I may not exactly be Donna Karan at the moment, but I noticed that all the buyers I've met, like, the real ones, like, from Nan Duskin, they all have this carriage, too. Like, well, if I were crude, like my ex-boyfriend, I'd say, like, they all have a stick up their ass, but I don't mean it like that. I mean, they have a way, like they're regal, or anchoring the national news, or something.

KATE: I don't know.

RISSA: I love it on you. I do.

KATE: Well, you've been right before.

RISSA: It's my job. And also discretion. I can keep a secret like nobody's business. You wouldn't believe what I know about my customers.

KATE: Really.

RISSA: No one you would know. Well, there is one.

KATE: You know something about someone I know.

RISSA: I shouldn't say.

KATE: No. Of course.

RISSA: But, if I did tell you, then you could tell me anything you wanted, really, because you'd have one on me. Because, if it ever got out about this person who, only I would know about this, although I didn't necessarily hear it from her... well, any chances I have to own this business would be gone.

KATE: You probably shouldn't say.

RISSA: No. But, I will if you want me to...

[*Change to* LINDA *and* MARIEL.]

LINDA: Mariel... stop crying...

MARIEL: I can't... I can't.

LINDA: Mariel... we're in a fitting room.

MARIEL: I just can't go on with my life like this. It's so empty. I'm such a nothing.

LINDA: Look... aside from how our lower bodies look in these mirrors there's really nothing wrong with either of our lives.

MARIEL: That's easy for you to say.

LINDA: Yes, it is.

MARIEL: You're a strong person. You were prepared for misery.

LINDA: Oh?

MARIEL: Ever since high school you knew you could never be happy. I mean, you would never read a book unless you were sure the author killed herself.

LINDA: You're a strong person, too.

MARIEL: I thought that if Gary and I got married everything would fall together for me.

LINDA: You did?

MARIEL: Well, no. But, I didn't know what else to do.

LINDA: You've been a child your whole life, Mariel.

MARIEL: At least I wasn't afraid to fall in love.

LINDA: I wasn't afraid to fall in love.

MARIEL: You still are. This one's not smart enough. That one's not good enough in bed.

LINDA: Those are the facts, Mariel.

MARIEL: I truly loved Gary when I married him.

LINDA: And look at all it's done for you.

MARIEL: What am I going to do? I can't even stand for him to touch me.

LINDA: I tried to warn you.

MARIEL: And I have nowhere to go.

LINDA: You can always come and live with me.

MARIEL: And be your wife?

LINDA: What does that mean?

MARIEL: Isn't that what you want? To have someone make your life nice for you the way Gary wants me to do that for him.

LINDA: That's ridiculous.

MARIEL: No, it isn't. You'd love to have someone cook for you and nurture you and make you feel like the big cheese.

LINDA: Is that a crime?

MARIEL: Well, it won't be me. I'm through earning my keep as a good girl.

LINDA: I'm sure I didn't ask you.

MARIEL: But, you want it. You want me to cook for you.

LINDA: Mariel, do you have some strange desire to cook for me?

MARIEL: I don't have the desire to cook for anyone.

LINDA: But you have the desire to poison someone.

MARIEL: Yes.

LINDA: Who?

MARIEL: You. And Gary.

LINDA: So, now the truth is out.

MARIEL: I guess it is.

LINDA: You completely resent me because you believe that I am superior to you. In taste, intellect, and lifestyle.

MARIEL: That's not the truth. The truth is I'm tired of being pushed around by powermongers.

LINDA: Oh. Well, in either case I think you'd better hurry and pay for that dress. We have lunch reservations.

[*Light change to* RISSA *and* KATE.]

RISSA: So, how old were you when you gave her up for adoption?

KATE: I was quite a bit older than you might imagine an unwed mother being.

RISSA: So, you were unwed.

KATE: I was only unwed to the child's father.

RISSA: But to Mr. Oliver you were...

KATE: Wed.

RISSA: Whoa.

KATE: And now he's gone. And there are no children.

RISSA: And you haven't seen her for all these years?

KATE: No.

RISSA: Didn't you wonder about her?

KATE: Sometimes I wondered. Sometimes I was obsessed. And sometimes I didn't think about her at all.

RISSA: Wow.

KATE: I probably shouldn't have told you this.

RISSA: Oh, no. It's good. Because, you know, I can help you find the right outfit.

KATE: Oh. So, now you don't think this is right?

RISSA: Well, I thought it was. Like, for a party. But to meet your daughter who you gave up for adoption, I don't think so.

KATE: It's too...

RISSA: Green. You need to wear something pink now, I would say. Yeah...I have the perfect dress...

KATE: Why do you say pink.

RISSA: Well, pink...It's soft, feminine. It'll make her feel more sorry for you. You want her to feel sorry for you because she's probably really pissed off right now.

KATE: Actually, she doesn't know yet.

RISSA: You didn't get in touch with her.

KATE: Not yet.

RISSA: Were you planning on just showing up at her doorstep and saying, like, hi, I'm your new Mom, how do you like my dress?

KATE: I hadn't thought it through, really.

RISSA: Try this. If you were my biological mother that's what I'd want you to wear.

KATE: Really?

RISSA: Yes.

KATE: You're very kind, Rissa.

RISSA: Me? Please, I'm a businesswoman.

KATE: You're a real person.

RISSA: Is that such an honor?

KATE: You really listen.

RISSA: I like my ladies to look good.

KATE: What about you? Do you have a close relationship to your mother?

RISSA: My mother? My mother is a saint.

KATE: That's nice.

RISSA: So, I completely take her for granted.

KATE: But, you love her.

RISSA: She's my mother.

KATE: She gave you life.

RISSA: But, I don't remember that.

KATE: Oh.

RISSA: You know how it is. Your mother. You need her when you're sick, or you got dumped, or you're broke, or some tragedy, event, or another. And, like, when everything is great for you you pretend your mother is, like, Sophia Loren, or somebody amazing like that, who would take you to the Cannes Film Festival. And she takes it from you 'cause she can still remember when you were cute, and you made her like a woodcut of your dog or something.

KATE: Oh, I see.

RISSA: Yeah, but you don't necessarily care that she had all this pain when you were born. I mean, you feel bad, but for the most part that's her problem.

KATE: Uh huh.

RISSA: If it had been up to you, you probably would have stayed where you were.

KATE: Right.

RISSA: So how did you find your daughter?

KATE: I just looked up her number. I always knew where she was.

RISSA: And all this time you never tried to reach her.

KATE: No.

RISSA: So, how come you want to now?

KATE: I don't know really.

RISSA: Well . . . I should stop asking so many questions anyway. People aren't supposed to be so interested in each other. You know.

KATE: I don't mind.

RISSA: It's just that, I don't know, for as far back as I can remember I always liked knowing other people's business.

KATE: I just hope she likes me, that's all.

RISSA: Yeah. What if you don't like her.

KATE: What?

RISSA: I mean what if she turns out to be nothing like you imagined, like, what if she's wild, or rude, or even dumb, or something.

KATE: I don't think so.

RISSA: You never know.

KATE: I really don't think so.

RISSA: So, what kind of relationship do you think you'll have with her?

KATE: What do you mean?

RISSA: I mean, are you gonna spend holidays with her, stuff like that?

KATE: I don't know.

RISSA: You're going to introduce her to your friends, kind of like bring her into society?

KATE: Well...I imagine that those aspects of her life are already defined.

RISSA: Oh. Is that what you imagine?

[*Light change to* TIA *and* KAHINE.]

TIA: I sent white light to my mother and father last night because they are going down the Nile.

KAHINE: Going down the Nile's not dangerous.

TIA: But they were going in, like, a gondola. It was my mother's whole thing.

KAHINE: Your mother's cool.

TIA: I hope they don't die or something.

KAHINE: My father might be coming to see my apartment this weekend.

TIA: Uh-huh. Has he ever seen it before?

KAHINE: No. But I sent him a picture of it.

TIA: When was the last time you saw him?

KAHINE: Umm . . . I think it was right after I burned down the dorm.

TIA: That was a while ago.

KAHINE: Yeah. But he calls a lot.

TIA: Well, he got you a great apartment.

KAHINE: What do you think of this?

TIA: I can't believe my parents are making me live with them again this year. I'm, like, the only one at school who doesn't have their own place. Why, because I'm sixteen? Well, too bad, too bad.

KAHINE: Tia! Tia! I asked you what you thought of these on me? I'm wearing these pants to show you and you're not looking at me. Why can't you look at me when I show you something?!

TIA: Kahine, Kahine . . . calm down . . . I'm looking at them. They look great. OK? Are you OK?

KAHINE: OK. I hate it when you do that.

TIA: I'm sorry.

KAHINE: I hate it when I ask you something, and you go right on to the next thing.

TIA: OK. I'm sorry.

KAHINE: I hate that.

TIA: I won't do it again.

KAHINE: Do you think these make me look fat?

TIA: Not at all.

KAHINE: 'Cause my dance teacher told me I looked fat.

TIA: That's bullshit.

KAHINE: I don't look fat?

TIA: Not at all.

KAHINE: Do I look good in them?

TIA: Excellent.

KAHINE: You sure?

TIA: Yes.

KAHINE: You swear?

TIA: Yes.

KAHINE: Even the lace?

TIA: They're perfect.

KAHINE: 'Cause they're really expensive.

TIA: So what?

KAHINE: Well...

TIA: You look beautiful in them, and William will think so, too!

KAHINE: OK. [*She takes them off.*]

TIA: What are you going to do?

KAHINE: I'm going to steal them.

[*Light change to* MARIEL *and* LINDA.]

MARIEL: Are you trying to tell me that you're a lesbian.

LINDA: I'm not trying to tell you anything. You're the one who's crying and telling me you can't go on.

MARIEL: With the marriage. Not go on in general. You're the depressed one. You're the pessimistic one.

LINDA: I'm not depressed.

MARIEL: Well, you're pessimistic.

LINDA: Yes. But I'm not unhappy about it.

MARIEL: So, why must you control me?

LINDA: Someone must.

MARIEL: Maybe you're really in love with me.

LINDA: Mariel...you are very confused.

MARIEL: Are you implying that I'm in love with you?

LINDA: I'm not implying anything.

MARIEL: Is that why I'm so dependent on your opinions?

LINDA: I don't know.

MARIEL: Is that why you could always make me lose my confidence?

LINDA: What confidence?

MARIEL: Is that why I got so jealous when you slept with Pamela's husband?

LINDA: I didn't know that made you jealous.

MARIEL: Well, it did somehow.

LINDA: You never told me that.

MARIEL: You spent all that time talking about Pamela. And her husband. And I thought... what's wrong with my husband?

LINDA: You were jealous because I didn't sleep with Gary?

MARIEL: Maybe.

LINDA: Oh, God.

MARIEL: Why? Did you sleep with Gary?

LINDA: Mariel...

MARIEL: Did you?

LINDA: What would you care if I did? You just said you can't stand him.

MARIEL: You did, didn't you?

LINDA: I thought we were trying to figure out if you were in love with me.

MARIEL: Oh, you must really think that I'm an idiot.

LINDA: No. I don't.

MARIEL: After all these years. Is that why you left your high powered job to come shopping with me, today? Because you feel guilty?

LINDA: I don't feel guilty.

MARIEL: Well, you wouldn't. You and your big important job.

LINDA: Oh. And now you're jealous of my job.

MARIEL: No, I'm not. I don't even know what it is.

LINDA: I'm a judge. I'm the youngest city judge to ever sit on the bench. There. Are you jealous, now?

MARIEL: You're very mean.

LINDA: Mariel, for once I'd like to have a conversation with you that doesn't involve men or clothes. For once, after being friends with you for eighteen years, I'd like to be acknowledged by you for my work, and I'd like you to stop using me as the mirror for all of your neuroses.

MARIEL: Is that what I do? I thought I was looking up to you.

LINDA: It's a use job.

MARIEL: I think you're the user.

LINDA: I don't think so. "Linda, how does this look on me? Linda, do I look fat in this?"

[*Fast change to* RISSA *and* KATE.]

RISSA: That's the dress for a mother.

KATE: You're certain I don't look fat?

[*Fast change to* TIA *and* KAHINE.]

TIA: Kahine. Don't do it.

KAHINE: Why not? Do they make me look fat?

TIA: No. Just don't take them!

KAHINE: But, I want to.

TIA: I don't want you to.

KAHINE: Why not?

TIA: Look . . . they cost two hundred dollars!

KAHINE: So?

TIA: So, that's a lot to steal.

KAHINE: So?

TIA: God, Kahine, I feel like we're on an ABC "After School Special". Don't steal the fucking pants, OK?

KAHINE: Fuck you, Tia! Don't be such a pussy for a change!

TIA: Don't be such a psycho case for a change.

KAHINE: I'm not a psycho case.

TIA: Oh, right, Kahine.

KAHINE: You think I'm a psycho case all of a sudden?

TIA: No, not all of a sudden.

KAHINE: Oh! You always thought I was a psycho case!

TIA: Well, Kahine, when you came into Modern with your wrists slashed, and bandaged with my old Danskins,™ then I had a clue.

KAHINE: You were crying in Modern.

TIA: I know!

KAHINE: I thought you really cared about me.

TIA: I did.

KAHINE: You didn't.

TIA: Yes, I did. But I still thought you were crazy.

KAHINE: You are shallow.

TIA: No, I'm not.

KAHINE: I thought we were both deep, but you are not deep.

TIA: Yes, I am. I'm deep.

KAHINE: You are not. You're shallow.

TIA: Kahine, I'm sorry. I don't want you to steal the pants. I don't want to get caught stealing. My mother shops in this store.

KAHINE: Your fucking shallow mother.

TIA: My mother is not shallow.

KAHINE: Your mother is an asshole.

TIA: At least I have one.

KAHINE: Did you think that saying that was going to make me not steal these pants?

[*Change to* RISSA *and* KATE.]

KATE: Well, I really needed to tell someone this. I'm glad you got it out of me.

RISSA: Well...

KATE: And I trust you. Maybe it's your earthiness. I don't know.

RISSA: My earthiness? You think I'm earthy?

KATE: You know. Your street sense. In many ways I've been very sheltered.

RISSA: Street sense? Do I sound like I come from the streets?

KATE: I don't mean it as an insult.

RISSA: Do you mean it as a compliment?

KATE: I mean it as an observation. I've never talked to anyone about this before.

RISSA: So, now you're talking to a salesgirl in a boutique.

KATE: But I think of you as more than that.

RISSA: But don't. 'Cause I'm proud of what I do.

KATE: I don't mean to patronize.

RISSA: But you should. You're a patron.

KATE: Look, I...

RISSA: No... it's my fault. I just watch alot of talk shows... I get this mixed up with that.

KATE: I would like to know what you think.

RISSA: Yeah?

KATE: Yes. What do you think she might want from me?

RISSA: Well... who doesn't fantasize about coming from money.

KATE: Does one?

RISSA: And having a fairy godmother come along and buy her her own store, and all. I mean, I fantasized that about you, and I'm not even your long lost daughter.

KATE: Is that something you want.

RISSA: It's why my mom plays the lottery.

KATE: Your own place.

RISSA: I'm not your daughter, am I?

KATE: You?

RISSA: Am I? Is that what you've been trying to tell me? Is that why you want to know what I think? You weren't really that interested in the secret that I told you about Damaris Warren and her affair with that archbishop, were you?

KATE: Well, yes, I was.

RISSA: I think you've been trying to tell me this for a long time haven't you, Mrs. Oliver? I always knew there was something between us. And you know how I'm always so interested in your parties, and how I wanted to please you when I made those lace collars for you? And how I look up to you. I mean, there's always been something there, hasn't there?

[KAHINE'S *frantic voice cuts through the action.*]

KAHINE: Hey...hey, salegirl!

RISSA: Uh-oh.

KAHINE: Look...I'm taking these pants with me? Did you hear me?

[MARIEL *and* LINDA *come out of their dressing room.*]

RISSA: Hey honey, just calm down, OK?

KAHINE: I'm taking these pants. And I'm not paying for them. What are you going to do?

RISSA: Those are leggings.

KAHINE: What?

RISSA: Those are leggings. Not pants.

KAHINE: Do they come with a top?

RISSA: Yes...

KAHINE: Well, I'm taking that, too.

TIA: Kahine, stop. You're going to get in a lot of trouble.

KAHINE: Don't start crying again, Tia.

MARIEL: That little girl looks insane.

LINDA: Dear, why don't you just calm down and stop screaming. We're in a very nice store.

KAHINE: Why don't I just kill myself? That's what you want, isn't it, Tia?

TIA: Kahine, you're my best friend. I just didn't want to get in trouble.

KAHINE: I hate you and your shallow world.

RISSA: Little girl, give me those leggings or I'm going to beat the shit out of you.

KAHINE: Go ahead.

[*She pulls a silverpoint pen out of her pocket.*]

TIA: That's my silverpoint! Did you take that from my bag, Kahine?

KAHINE: Yes! I liked it, so I took it.

TIA: You dropped out of art 'cause you were bored doing silverpoint, and then you stole my silverpoint!

KAHINE: I liked it.

TIA: Give it back! And give back the leggings!

KATE: I should really go, Rissa dear. Is there a back entrance?

RISSA: One second, Mrs. Oliver.

MARIEL: I know how you feel little girl.

KAHINE: You don't know anything about this. This is between me and my enemy.

TIA: I'm not your enemy.

KAHINE: My traitor!

TIA: I'm not a traitor! Stop saying bad things about me!

KAHINE: Stop crying, traitor!

TIA: I didn't do anything. I just told her not to steal the pants. Leggings.

KATE: I really have to go. If something should happen here it wouldn't be good for me...I mean...

RISSA: I don't think anyone should move right now, Mrs. Oliver.

MARIEL: Give me that little knife now. You could hurt yourself.

KAHINE: It's not a knife. It's a silverpoint. It's used for drawing.

MARIEL: But it's sharp. I don't want you to hurt yourself.

KAHINE: Why not?

MARIEL: Because ... you're cute.

TIA: I always thought you were cute. I always thought you were cuter than me!

MARIEL: Just try to calm down. Poor thing.

LINDA: Mariel ... why don't you let the store handle this?

MARIEL: Who's the store?

RISSA: I'm the store. But, if you can calm this kid down and get her out of here, fine.

LINDA: I really don't think she's going to hurt herself with that ball-point pen, or whatever it is.

[KAHINE, *realizing she has lost some impact, grabs a pair of scissors near the cash register.*]

RISSA: Shit.

KATE: This is awful.

RISSA: This is what kids are like sometimes, Mrs. Oliver. You gotta be prepared for anything. You know?

KATE: But, I'm not good in these sorts of situations. I mean, what's the protocol?

RISSA: There is no protocol when children are involved. It's all about survival.

KATE: Oh, my ...

LINDA: Keep your distance, Mariel.

MARIEL: No.

[KAHINE *starts to lose her balance. She grabs her stomach and gets shakier.*]

TIA: She only ate ketchup and water for lunch. And for dinner she drinks a Slimfast milkshake. And then she has a cigarette 'cause she wants to be a dancer, and I keep telling her to eat, but I have to do homework, and my Mom makes me get off the phone by ten, and there's only so much I can do for her 'cause she already tried to kill herself twice, and her stupid boyfriend William is an arsonist! There, and if you think I'm a traitor then now I am one, but it's only because I love you, and you're so fucked up.

MARIEL: She's probably all malnourished and everything.

LINDA: Oh, God.

KAHINE: Don't call my father.

TIA: Your father?

KAHINE: You better not call him.

TIA: I can't, he's in Tokyo or someplace.

MARIEL: I'm sure your father loves you very much.

KAHINE: How would you know?

MARIEL: Men always love their daughters. It's their wives they have problems with.

KAHINE: I just don't want him to be called.

MARIEL: Well, we're going to have to call him.

RISSA: You're going to call Japan on my phone?

MARIEL: I'll use my card.

RISSA: Fuck it. Just call direct. Where's he staying, and if you don't tell us I'll turn those scissors around and cut all the perm out of your head.

TIA: I remember! He's at the Tokyo Sheraton!

KAHINE: Marriot.

MARIEL: Yes, Operator, how do I place an overseas call to Japan? . . . I do?

RISSA: What?

MARIEL: Can you believe in this day and age I have to wait for an open line?

RISSA: See that, Mrs. Oliver? And we had trouble with that Osaki zipper! Even the Japanese have their problems. Mrs. Oliver?

[*She is gone.*]

LINDA: This is an excellent way to lose customers.

RISSA: Yeah. It is.

[KAHINE *stumbles.*]

TIA: Here! I've got them! I've got the scissors.

RISSA: Give me the phone. I'm calling the police.

LINDA: Good. Now, let's get out of here.

TIA: Please, don't call the police.

MARIEL: Please. I'm waiting for the overseas operator.

[KAHINE *passes out.*]

LINDA: Oh, for God's sake.

TIA: See? I told you she doesn't eat anything!

RISSA: Well, sit her the hell down. I've got a hoagie.

TIA: Kahine . . . you've got to eat some of the ladie's hoagie!

LINDA: Look . . . I've got to get back to work. Are you coming out to lunch with me?

MARIEL: I don't think so.

LINDA: What are you going to do, stay here by the phone for this child?

MARIEL: Yes. For the moment.

LINDA: Mariel . . . this not the ASPCA.

MARIEL: I want to do this.

LINDA: But we have lunch plans.

MARIEL: Not anymore. I don't feel like lunch.

LINDA: Oh? What do you feel like?

MARIEL: I feel like . . . getting divorced. And having a baby.

LINDA: That's rational.

MARIEL: I know I don't feel like sitting somewhere and clamoring for your attention.

LINDA: Is that what you think you do?

MARIEL: Yes. I clamor.

LINDA: And what do I do?

MARIEL: You divvy out. You divvy out. And I clamor.

LINDA: Well, then... Can I call you?

MARIEL: Can you?

LINDA: Should I? I mean, can I call you, or how do you want to leave this, Mariel? I mean are we leaving this, Mariel? Because I don't really think I could do without this... without your friendship... Oh... what am I saying? I'll just be at work, and you can call me if you want to. Do you think you'll want to?

MARIEL: Yes. I think I'll want to.

LINDA: Well, good then. Then, I'll wait. To hear from you.

[LINDA *exits*.]

RISSA: OK? You're all right now?

KAHINE: That was a good hoagie.

RISSA: Yeah?

KAHINE: Uh-huh.

RISSA: Well, I get the meats down on Ninth Street. But I think the magic is in the olive oil. You can get anything down there. Detergent, cannolis, anything you need.

TIA: We'll have to go there sometime, right Kahine? We love to shop.

KAHINE: OK.

TIA: Kahine, you don't really think I'm shallow, do you? Like you said? 'Cause I would just die if you thought I was shallow.

KAHINE: No.

TIA: Kahine's my best friend. That's why I get so worried when she's starving.

RISSA: I can understand that.

MARIEL: Oh ... hello ... They're going to put me through. Do you want to talk to your father?

KAHINE: Me?

MARIEL: Would you like me to? To explain the situation? I can tell him that you were furious and hysterical. And that you needed to be understood. And listened to. And taken seriously, but by him in particular. That your rather frenetic behavior was a last ditch effort to get his attention, but that luckily you have a lot of support, and that you appreciate that support very much. Shall I tell him all of that?

KAHINE: No.

MARIEL: Well, what if I just give you a ride home, then. I have a driver.

KAHINE: That's cool.

TIA: That is so cool.

MARIEL: Hello? Oh no, operator. You can just cancel that call.

RISSA: There, now. Everybody's OK. And you all have nice outfits. So there can't be anything to get so upset about, right?

TIA: Right.

RISSA: Right. So ... sometimes things get a little crazy when you're trying on clothes. It just does it to you, sometimes. So, what are you gonna do?

END OF PLAY

Mlada Imaginaire
adapted from the French by Michael Feingold

SCRIBE'S PARADOX, OR
THE MECHANICAL RABBIT

MICHAEL FEINGOLD

Michael Feingold has worked in the theatre for more than twenty years as a critic, playwright, translator, lyricist, director, dramaturg, and literary manager. A graduate of Columbia University and the Yale School of Drama, he is best known as the chief theatre critic for *The Village Voice*. His column has won him a Guggenheim Fellowship and the American Book Awards' Walter Lowenfels Prize in criticism. His articles have also appeared in many other magazines and newspapers.

Feingold's alternate career in the theatre itself began in 1970, when he was named Literary Manager of the newly formed Yale Repertory Theatre, a post he held for seven years. For YRT he directed numerous staged readings, wrote and/or directed children's shows with student actors (including such future luminaries as Meryl Streep, Sigourney Weaver, Chris Durang, and Albert Innaurato), and provided translations for many of the Rep's most significant productions, including the Brecht/Weill *Rise and Fall of Mahagonny*, *Little Mahagonny*, and *Happy End*; Molière's *Bourgeois Gentleman*; Diderot's *Rameau's Nephew*; Ibsen's *When We Dead Awaken*; and the Dostoyevsky/Camus *Possessed*, staged by Andrzej Wajda. He subsequently became Literary Director of the Guthrie Theater in Minneapolis, followed by a stint as Literary Manager of the American Repertory Theatre in Cambridge, Massachusettes.

In New York, he has directed for the American Place Theatre, Circle Rep, Manhattan Theatre Club, and the WPA theatre, among others. His translations have been heard in many of the above theatres, as well as at La Mama, the Public Theatre, Theatre Ubu, the Classic Stage Company, and on Broadway (*Happy End* with Meryl Streep and Christopher Lloyd, and the recent *Three Penny Opera* starring Sting and Maureen McGovern). His translations of opera, light opera, and songs by composers from Offenbach and Schumann to Penderecki have been heard at the Santa Fe, San Francisco, and Los Angeles opera houses, and in many concert halls.

Currently, Feingold teaches classic drama to playwriting students at New York University's Tisch School of the Arts, and a course in collaboration for directing and dramaturgy students at Columbia University's Hammerstein Center. His new translation of *The Firebugs* by Max Frisch was done at the Guthrie Theatre in Minneapolis, Minnesota in August 1995, and *When Ladies Battle*, his translation of the Scribe play, was produced by the Pearl Theatre, off-Broadway, in January 1996.

CHARACTERS

ORFIN — A playwright

A FEMALE THEATREGOER

A PROFESSOR

MADAME DU CAMP — An actress

RANDEAU — A stage director

SCENE: *Paris. The lobby of the Theatre des Somnambules, where* ORFIN'S *latest play is running.*

TIME: *1895. Just after a performance.*

FEMALE THEATREGOER: [*Coming out of the auditorium and approaching* ORFIN.] Excuse me, but aren't you Monsieur Orfin?

ORFIN: Are you a debt collector?

FEMALE THEATREGOER: What an idea! Of course not!

ORFIN: In that case, I am Orfin, at your service.

FEMALE THEATREGOER: I thought so! Your play is very good. I enjoyed it immensely.

ORFIN: Thank you. I hope you will tell all your friends.

FEMALE THEATREGOER: I will, but— [*Looking around cautiously, lowering her voice.*] —it is not well made.

ORFIN: I beg your pardon?

FEMALE THEATREGOER: Your play is not a well-made play.

ORFIN: [*Somewhat nettled.*] It was made well enough for you to enjoy it.

FEMALE THEATREGOER: Oh, you know what I mean.

ORFIN: I'm not at all sure.

FEMALE THEATREGOER: It isn't well constructed.

ORFIN: Ah, you mean like the plays of Monsieur Scribe and Monsieur Sardou?

FEMALE THEATREGOER: Yes, exactly. There is no central figure trapped between two untenable choices. There is no clever antagonist to counter each of the central figure's attempts to escape from this situation.

ORFIN: No quid pro quo, you mean?

FEMALE THEATREGOER: That is precisely what I mean. For instance, take *A Glass of Water*—

ORFIN: I'm not thirsty, thank you.

FEMALE THEATREGOER: Oh, don't be silly. I mean Monsieur Scribe's famous play of that name.

ORFIN: Ah, yes. *The Glass of Water*. And what about it?

FEMALE THEATREGOER: Each of the characters is in one of these untenable dilemmas. Each move brings one side or the other up against a countermove. The exposition is all in the first act, the climax in the third, the resolution in the fifth.

ORFIN: Yes, Monsieur Scribe is very clever about these things.

FEMALE THEATREGOER: But your play has no such structure.

ORFIN: Dear lady, my play is in one scene. Under the circumstances, it could hardly resolve in its fifth act.

FEMALE THEATREGOER: But it could follow a pattern of rising action. It could have an untenable dilemma, and a series of quid pro quo maneuvers.

ORFIN: I find my temper rising in lieu of the action; your demands make talking to you an untenable dilemma. If you go on in this manner, my maneuver will simply be to walk away.

FEMALE THEATREGOER: But I am only an innocent audience member who wants to know more.

ORFIN: Your attitude suggests to me that you lost your innocence long ago. [*She gasps.*] Aesthetically speaking, I mean.

PROFESSOR: [*Coming up to them.*] Madame, is this man bothering you?

ORFIN: On the contrary: The lady is doing her best to bother me.

PROFESSOR: I warn you, sir, if you insult her again, you will have to deal with me.

ORFIN: And who, may I ask, will I then be dealing with?

PROFESSOR: [*Bowing.*] I am Kaltfisch, Professor of Aesthetics at the University of Lyon.

ORFIN: May I suggest, Professor, that Lyon's aesthetics need considerably more reforming than mine.

PROFESSOR: Sir, if your aesthetics include harassing innocent women in theatre lobbies—

ORFIN: You came in late, Professor. I am the author of the play being presented here. The lady is harassing me about my lack of structural sense.

PROFESSOR: [*Clasping his hands.*] My dear fellow, can you ever forgive me! Your play is simply splendid!

FEMALE THEATREGOER: [*Perturbed.*] But Professor—

PROFESSOR: [*Ignoring the interruption.*] You do away with all these antiquated hoodoos about "structure." No contrivance, no manipulation, no elaborately rigged-up system of alliances and counter-alliances—just a person who does something and its consequences. That is drama at its purest. None of the nonsense of Scribe, Sardou, Dumas fils, Augier, Feuillet, and so forth.

ORFIN: I appreciate your enthusiasm, Professor, but I hope you will let me put in a word in defense of my colleagues. My own approach is different from theirs—this is a changing world we live in—but I admire and even enjoy their contrivances, as you call them. I love to watch the little machines whirl and click into place as these not-quite believable characters maneuver their way from one situation to another. You are quite right to say that it is not the living drama, which is what I prefer, but it is the pattern of drama, and we are all beholden to the pattern, so we must respect it.

MADAME DU CAMP: [*Sweeping up, grandly dressed.*] Orfy, my love, we've been looking for you all over the theatre.

ORFIN: Jeanne, please let me introduce—

FEMALE THEATREGOER: Oh, Madame, what a magnificent performance!

MADAME DU CAMP: Thank you.

FEMALE THEATREGOER: [*Extending her program to be signed.*] You are the most wonderful actress of our century! That red dress! And the way you looked at him when he accused you of infidelity with the chauffeur!

MADAME DU CAMP: [*Laughing as she signs program with an elaborate flourish.*] Oh, well, Duse will probably find some even more cunning way of doing that in the Italian version. [*To* ORFIN.] Remember her in the confession scene of *The Princess of Baghdad?* With the little boy? That was divine!

ORFIN: [*Imitating Duse folding the child's hands over his heart.*] I remember. "I have been faithful! I swear it! *Lo giuro!*" It was brilliant... though not half so brilliant as you, my dear.

MADAME DU CAMP: Well, you'll have to write me something brilliant like that to do in your next. Which had better be soon, Orfy. That's why I've been trying to find you. We're taking this play off. It's not going to run. The new one must be ready in five weeks.

ORFIN: But everyone loves you in this! I love you in this! You've never been more wonderful. And this is the most original thing I've ever written.

MADAME DU CAMP: Oh, Orfy, don't be banal. I mean— [*Looking at* PROFESSOR *and* FEMALE THEATREGOER.] —you'll forgive my saying this in front of your relatives from the country, but—this play doesn't give me a chance. I only get one costume change, I only have two entrances. I don't get an exit because the curtain comes down for intermission with me still onstage—

ORFIN: [*Testily.*] Talk to Randeau about that. I told him you should exit before it came down.

MADAME DU CAMP: Oh, Orfy, honey, that isn't the point. I have no big scenes!

ORFIN: No big scenes! What about the confrontation scene! This woman has just been telling you how wonderful you were in it.

MADAME DU CAMP: I'm wonderful, I know, but the scene has no "build." I need to feel that roller-coaster of motion sweeping me along. I can do my part, but there's nothing hanging over my head, no extra push. You look back at the classics, sweetie. Look at Scribe—

ORFIN: Scribe! You want me to write like Scribe!

MADAME DU CAMP: Well, I'll tell you, he never wrote a woman a weak role. I come out there in *When Ladies Battle*, or *Adrienne Lecouvreur*, and I know exactly what's going on. I have something I want, I have a secret I must conceal, I have an enemy whose maneuvers against me are all announced openly, step by step, so that I can take steps to counter them, I get three or four costume changes, the audience sees me go from happy to sad to hysterical in an instant, and every scene has a strong entrance, a crushing last line, and one or two laughs. Now how can you top that?

ORFIN: [*Through clenched teeth.*] In *Adrienne Lecouvreur* you have to die by sniffing poisoned violets. How can I take that seriously?

MADAME DU CAMP: Well, it doesn't have to be Scribe. In those days they all knew how to do it. Take Augier for instance, *Olympia's Marriage*—

ORFIN: In *Olympia's Marriage* the elderly judge rescues his son from marriage to the ex-courtesan by shooting you, I mean her. It's absurd. A Paris audience would laugh it off the stage today.

MADAME DU CAMP: I don't know, I've been thinking of reviving it— it's very popular in America just now.

ORFIN: America! We're talking about civilization here, not the savage tribes.

MADAME DU CAMP: Wait till you see my Act III wedding dress. And Randeau's worked out something spectacular for my death scene.

ORFIN: [*Bitterly.*] So this is my fate! To be replaced by a mechanical rabbit from fifty years ago!

MADAME DU CAMP: Oh, don't take it so hard, my cabbage. I want to do your next one immediately after. The Augier revival is just to give you time to write it. And practice the old pattern a little. We want you to write a play that's really well made, so everyone will love it. We know you can do it.

ORFIN: Yes, but do I want to? The world's not well-made. Those plays are old, artificial postures.

MADAME DU CAMP: [*Laughing.*] Yes, darling. That's why we love them. Reality is depressing—more so every year. People come to the theatre for escape. They need artifice—the more artificial the better.

ORFIN: Why am I always at your mercy this way?

MADAME DU CAMP: [*Simply.*] You adore me.

ORFIN: Yes. And your husband owns the theatre.

MADAME DU CAMP: Oh, hush. Don't talk about my husband, or these people will suspect some kind of marital intrigue. [*Looking at* PROFESSOR *and* FEMALE THEATREGOER, *who have been watching with rapt attention.*] Who are they, anyway?

PROFESSOR: [*Bowing.*] Kaltfisch, University of Lyon.

MADAME DU CAMP: Oh, Professor! How lovely to see you. Goodness, in this flurry I almost forgot all about our appointment. Has the Augier family approved our terms?

PROFESSOR: [*Touching his breast pocket.*] I have the contract here, Madame, whenever you are ready.

ORFIN: [*Agog.*] You praise my new aesthetic, and then you negotiate for Augier, most hackneyed of the old "well-made" playwrights?

PROFESSOR: The old must be given its chance, Monsieur, before the new sweeps it away.

FEMALE THEATREGOER: [*Who has edged over to* MADAME DU CAMP.] I can't tell you how excited I am! I saw Rejane play Olympia when I was a little girl. To think of seeing you in it now!

MADAME DU CAMP: [*Joshing.*] It will make you feel like a little girl all over again. [*They laugh together.*] Would you like a tour of our theatre? Come, I'll show you around. Come, Professor.

PROFESSOR: With pleasure.

[*They go off, leaving* ORFIN *alone in the now deserted lobby. Pause. Then* RANDEAU, *the director, comes up to him.*]

RANDEAU: Don't be downhearted.

ORFIN: Any special reason why not?

RANDEAU: You've triumphed. Everyone is talking about your play.

ORFIN: But, apparently, no one is coming to see it.

RANDEAU: That's all right. Let them come and see Augier for a while. They all know the terms have changed. The old tricks have been exposed as tricks. In the future, plays like yours will be enjoyed as plays. And the old plays will be enjoyed the way you and I enjoy them, for the pleasure of their trickery.

ORFIN: You make the future sound very just.

RANDEAU: It's a blind sort of justice, true, but in art it's the only kind we get. Anyway, you won't lose money by this.

ORFIN: I won't.

RANDEAU: I need someone to adapt the Augier script. His tricks are a little staler than Scribe's.

ORFIN: Won't the Professor object?

RANDEAU: You don't think professors ever really know their subject, do you? Come on, let's go for a drink and I'll tell you what I want done. We can go to that new place in Montmartre, where the painters hang out—the Lapin Agile.

ORFIN: All right, we'll go to the Lively Rabbit and try to wake up the mechanical one.

RANDEAU: That's the spirit! You'll write a well-made play yet.

ORFIN: [*Looking back to where* MADAME DU CAMP *has exited as he follows* RANDEAU *out.*] I already have. [*He exits dramatically.*]

CURTAIN

Janusz Glowacki

Translated by
Zuza Glowacka

HOME SECTION

JANUSZ GLOWACKI

Janusz Glowacki was born in Poland and graduated from Warsaw University. He has since worked as a playwright, screenwriter, novelist, short story writer, and essayist, and is the author of seven plays, ten books, six screenplays, and four produced movies, one of which, *Hunting Flies*, was directed by Andrzej Wajda.

In August 1980, during the strike in Gdansk shipyard which resulted in the birth of Solidarity, Januaz Glowacki spent time with the striking workers. From that experience he wrote the novel *Give Us This Day*. The novel, censored in Poland, was published underground in 1981 and all around the world soon after.

In December 1981, Mr. Glowacki was attending the opening of his play *Cinders* at the Royal Court Theatre in London. While he was there, martial law was declared in Poland. He decided not to return to his country and instead moved to New York. In 1984, *Cinders* was produced by Joseph Papp at the New York Shakespeare Festival and received Premio Molliere's Award as the best production of 1986 for its Buenos Aires appearance.

This was followed by the tragi-comedy *Fortinbras Gets Drunk* (1986), a macabre retelling of Hamlet from the Norwegian point of view, and the critically acclaimed *Hunting Cockroaches*. The latter was produced at the Manhattan Theatre Club in 1987 (starring Dianne Wiest and Ron Silver, and directed by Arthur Penn), at the Mark Taper Forum (starring Swoosie Kurtz and Malcolm McDowell), and by more than fifty other professional theatres across the U.S. It was cited by the American Theatre Critics Association as an Outstanding New Play in 1986, and received the Hollywood Drama Logue Critics Award. *Time Magazine*, among others, named the play as one of the ten best of the year.

His latest play, *Antigone In New York*, was produced at Arena Stage in Washington, D.C., in 1993. *Time Magazine* called it, too, one of the best ten plays of the year. The play was awarded Grand Prix at the Wroclaw Biennale of Contemporary Polish Plays in 1994.

Janusz Glowacki is the recipient of the National Endowment for the Arts Playwriting Fellowship, the Guggenheim Fellowship, Jurzykowski Foundation and Drama League of New York Playwriting Award.

CHARACTERS

WITEK

OLEK

PLAYWRIGHT

The stage is dark. The sound of Chopin's "Grand Polonaise in A Flat" is heard. A light turns on. The music fades. The stage setting is that of a typical living room on Fifth Avenue. Arm chairs, two Tiffany lamps, a sofa, a Persian rug, coffee table, etc. The stage is divided in two by two expensive doors which are closed at the moment. On stage right there is an entrance which connects the living room to the remaining rooms in the apartment. At this time, there aren't any people on stage. From backstage we hear loud noises of furniture being moved around, and men's voices.

WITEK: [*Offstage.*] Drop it here...

OLEK: [*Offstage.*] Move it here...

[An extremely loud crash followed by cursing is heard. Two renovating men enter the stage. They are carrying painting materials and a ladder. The first man, WITEK, *is talkative; the second,* OLEK, *is a big man, and is in a philosophical mood which is the usual case when a person is hungover. The third member of the crew is presently working in the maid's room; he is not seen on stage. They are all Polish immigrants. The specialty of Polish-Americans is renovating apartments, as the Korean specialty is running grocery stores.* WITEK *and* OLEK *are very professionally preparing the living room to be painted. They are stacking things in the middle of the room, covering with a white sheet, and putting some sheets on the floor. Afterwards, they begin their painting job. From the moment they entered the stage they have been talking continually.]*

OLEK: So you did it?

WITEK: I did it

OLEK: You put it on.

WITEK: I put it on.

OLEK: I wouldn't have put it on if I were you.

WITEK: Why not?

OLEK: It's a mortal sin, the Pope made that perfectly clear.

WITEK: I put it on.

OLEK: And...?

WITEK: And then she told me to put on another one.

OLEK: Why?

WITEK: Just in case.

OLEK: Did you do it?

WITEK: Absolutely not.

OLEK: You were absolutely right.

WITEK: Actually, I only had one.

OLEK: Thanks God. And...?

WITEK: And nothing. I put on my clothes and left. Watch it! You're spilling the paint.

[*From backstage, a loud noise is heard, as though a heavy object was just dropped. The noise comes from the room in which the third worker is moving furniture.*]

WITEK: [*Yells in his direction.*] What the fuck are you doing!

OLEK: What the fuck did they send us this guy for?

WITEK: It was Maciek's idea.

OLEK: Why? So I can share my money with this asshole.

WITEK: I told you, he used to be famous in Poland, Maciek liked one of his plays.

OLEK: What was it called?

WITEK: Uhhhh...*Skating On Thin Ice*. No. Wait. *A Polar Bear in Warsaw*. No. *Good-Bye Gulak*. No. *Hello Prague*. No... Something.

OLEK: I don't like playwrights myself. One day I went to a bar in Poland, met a playwright, and before I knew it, I was sentenced to three years in prison.

WITEK: He doesn't write for the police. He writes for the theater.

OLEK: Same thing! Witek, you are an experienced man.

WITEK: Sure. I've been working six years on this stuff.

OLEK: That's what I mean. So what do you think? Can women grow back their hair.

WITEK: What do you mean?

OLEK: [*Pointing.*] On the head.

WITEK: Never heard anything about it.

OLEK: Me neither. God, I'm tired... I worked my ass off. This is the fifth room today.

WITEK: Only three left.

OLEK: Three rooms. Shit!

WITEK: [*Proudly.*] This is not Brooklyn, this is Fifth Avenue. Two rooms left and the maid's room.

OLEK: What's a maid's room?

[*Again a crash is heard from backstage.*]

WITEK: That's the one, the playwright is fucking up. [*With a nostalgic smile.*] Olek?

OLEK: What?

WITEK: Is your father dead?

OLEK: Alive, why?

WITEK: Where is he?

OLEK: Where is he supposed to be? In Zelazowa Wola, of course.

WITEK: [*Deeply moved.*] Olek ?

OLEK: What ?

WITEK: Did your father ever dream ?

OLEK: About what?

WITEK: About you, his son Olek, renovating five bedroom apartments on Fifth Avenue. In New York City?

OLEK: My father wanted me to be a pianist.

WITEK: Pianist?

OLEK: Pianist. All of the fathers in our neighborhood wanted their sons to become pianists.

WITEK: Why?

OLEK: Because one man from Zelazowa Wola made a lot of money with the help of his piano.

WITEK: What's his name?

OLEK: Chopin.

WITEK: Yah, I heard of him, but I also heard that the money he made wasn't good for shit. He lived with some old French bitch, and fucked her for food.

OLEK: [*Surprised.*] Really? My father never mentioned that.

WITEK: Hey Olek! what the fuck you doing?

OLEK: Anyway, I wasn't very good at the piano. [*Looking at the wall.*] Don't worry, I'll fix it...

WITEK: We should roll up this carpet.

OLEK: Why the fuck roll it? It looks like shit.

WITEK: Because it's a Persian.

OLEK: So what ?

WITEK: A Persian has to look like shit, that's its quality. One Russian told me that he and his grandmother used to work fucking up new carpets to make them look like authentic Persian shit. They stomped on the carpet non-stop all day, and got three dollars per hour, each, for stomping.

OLEK: There is no shit in the world I would stomp on for three dollars an hour. [*Pointing to his head.*] And when a woman falls in love?

WITEK: What?

OLEK: Doesn't it grow back then?

WITEK: Oh, I don't know...

OLEK: Me, neither.

[*From backstage an even louder noise, like that of a book shelf crashing against the ground is heard.*]

OLEK: The bookcase.

WITEK: No, I think it's that big Picasso.

OLEK: Aha...This playwright of yours.

WITEK: What?

OLEK: I don't trust him.

WITEK: You said that already.

OLEK: I'm not talking about him being a squealer right now, it's just that objects don't get along very well with him.

WITEK: Naa, he's just sloppy, has two left hands.

OLEK: That's not what I mean.

WITEK: So what do you mean?

OLEK: There was this woman.

WITEK: What woman?

OLEK: In Zelazowa Wola.

WITEK: A pianist?

OLEK: No, whatever she touched fell apart, like my new chair. And then it turned out that she was Lisbonian.

WITEK: You mean, lesbian.

OLEK: That's what I said. You can deceive a man but a chair, forget it. [Pointing backstage.] And he is pro-condoms.

WITEK: I'm pro, too.

OLEK: You're a different story. Besides, you had only one, and he carries the whole pack in his pocket.

WITEK: How do you know? Did you search his pockets?

OLEK: Of course. If I don't trust someone I search his pocket.

WITEK: You are a thief.

OLEK: I didn't take them. I only put holes in them.

WITEK: Why?

OLEK: To save his soul ... with a nail. He should be grateful.

WITEK: Olek, if I ever catch you touching my condoms ...

OLEK: Fine, but you'll go to hell. [OLEK is taking a painting down from the wall. A huge hole is seen.]
        Aha, you see ... ?

WITEK: What?

OLEK: A hole.

WITEK: So what? There probably was a safe here.

OLEK: Maybe yes, maybe no.

[*Again a terrible noise from backstage.*]

WITEK: Maciek said they almost produced his play on Broadway. You know, something about Russia being ruled by the Mafia, who are the communists who used to shoot workers.

OLEK: But they are not shooting workers any more.

WITEK: But they could start shooting any time. And they promised him that immediately after they start shooting, his play will be reconsidered.

OLEK: But they're already shooting in Chechnya.

WITEK: But Chechnya doesn't count. On the legs, yes.

OLEK: What?

WITEK: Yes. It grows back on the legs.

OLEK: Ahhh ... I'm not talking about the legs. I only wanna know about the head.

[*Again a noise is heard.*]

WITEK: Motherfucker! He did it again. Have you got any paper?

OLEK: Only this. [*He takes out from his pocket a book, hands it to* WITEK.]

WITEK: [*Reads it.*] "How To Seduce a Stewardess." [*He tears off the cover of the book, and a few pages, slaps it on the wall, and paints over it. The cover slowly slips off of the wall.*]

WITEK: I should spit on it first. [*Glues the cover to the wall.*]

OLEK: I'm sure that if Chopin was born 100 years later and came to America he would have been a big hit.

[*Helps him with the gluing.*]

OLEK: It's much easier to make it here as a pianist than as a construction worker. Because when you play the piano nobody hears your accent.

WITEK: When Maciek came here six years ago, he didn't speak a word of English and had five dollars in his pocket. And now, you see how beautifully he speaks; everybody thinks he was born in

Brooklyn. [*He finishes fixing the hole.*] And now put some paint on it, but be careful.

OLEK: [*Painting the newspaper.*] Aha!

WITEK: Maciek has become a very important person. A week ago I met two guys at his apartment, both in white suits, black shirts, white ties, black socks, white shoes, black hats, Rolexes, and on every finger they had a golden ring. WASPs from the Upper East Side. And you know what they were talking about?

OLEK: What?

WITEK: That the quality of food on the Concord has gotten worse.

OLEK: Has it?

WITEK: How the fuck I should know. I don't fly the Concord. And you know who I met later in the hallway?

OLEK: Who?

WITEK: My wife, Kasia.

OLEK: Your wife?

WITEK: Yeah.

OLEK: I thought she left you.

WITEK: Of course. Do you really think she is stupid enough to stay with me? Maciek introduced her to the most sophisticated millionaires. She is one of them, now.

OLEK: Did you talk to her?

WITEK: [*Proud of his wife.*] Do you really think she is stupid enough to talk to me? She drives a Jaguar, all thanks to Maciek.

OLEK: When did she leave you?

WITEK: A year ago. It's all because of my fucking mother. You know, every night after dinner, she locked Kasia up in the room. And this one time she forgot. And the bitch ran away. But, she loved me. Like crazy. Especially when I came to take her from Poland. I mean, I told her I had a penthouse with a doorman...

OLEK: Why did you say that ?

WITEK: Why? Why? Because I loved her. She wouldn't have married me without a doorman.

OLEK: Maybe she found out you are gay.

WITEK: What? Me? Gay?

OLEK: Well, you did fuck me.

WITEK: Well... well, it was a misunderstanding. We talked about it already. I was sure you were gay. I just wanted to be nice. You are the one who started with that thing.

OLEK: Only because they told me in Warsaw that all men in New York are gay, so... I wanted to fit in. I didn't want you to think that I am stupid or anything... You know what ?

WITEK: What?

OLEK: A week ago I met a woman, Zosia. She has beautiful bowed legs like iron arches. She can strangle a dog with these legs.

WITEK: Does she live in Greenpoint, somewhere between McGuinnes and Manhattan Avenue, and have blond hair?

OLEK: No. On Calyer Street and she is bald like an American eagle. And all female from Zakopane are bald. Her mother, her grandmother, two cows. It's because of Lenin.

WITEK: Why?

OLEK: I don't know why.

WITEK: Aha. Give this spot one more touch.

OLEK: And she never asked me to wear this [*Pointing to his crotch.*]

WITEK: No?

OLEK: No?

WITEK: What if she got pregnant.

OLEK: Just yesterday, I asked her about that.

WITEK: And what?

OLEK: [*Smiling, proud of Zosia.*] She said that she would drown herself in the Hudson River.

WITEK: This is the kind of women I like.

OLEK: And she really takes care of men. When I sleep at her house she always puts two glasses next to my bed: one full, in case I am thirsty, and one empty in case I'm not. Here are some photos of her. [*He shows the pictures to* WITEK.] Here she is wearing a hat, and here she is bald.

WITEK: I like her better with the hat. Okay, let's start the other room. [OLEK *opens the door to another room and bumps into something unusual. We notice two legs of a man who hanged himself.*]

OLEK: I think I should marry her.

WITEK: So, do it.

OLEK: Shit.

WITEK: What?

OLEK: Her mother. She will never accept me. [*With no emotion at all.*] Someone is hanging here.

WITEK: I can see. Why won't she accept you?

[*They continue talking, scrutinizing the body.*]

OLEK: You know, her mom was once on TV and she is such a snob. But Zosia is completely different. What do you think? Who is he?

WITEK: How the fuck am I supposed to know.

OLEK: They showed her mother on "Primetime" as the only woman horse-carriage driver in Central Park.

WITEK: Oh, yeah. I remember that.

OLEK: [*Sadly.*] You see? You see? She's famous.

WITEK: But they only put her on because she whipped her horse to death.

OLEK: [*Proudly.*] You see? She is strong . . . What do you think? Is he Polish?

WITEK: Nah

OLEK: Jewish?

WITEK: Nah.

OLEK: Mexican?

WITEK: Why Mexican? He's got blond hair.

OLEK: I'm just talking. It helps me think.

WITEK: Anyway, what's the difference?

OLEK: It's a big difference. Yesterday in Greenpoint, they beat up this Indian—but by mistake. They thought he was a gypsy.

WITEK: Uh huh.

OLEK: But then they explained everything to him, and he completely understood. He said he would have done the same thing. [*Pointing to the body.*] How'd he get in here.

WITEK: Because look at the way he's dressed. Clean collar, silk tie, and polished shoes...Of course the doorman was going to let him in. I told you you have to dress better. In New York, do you know what is the most important thing?

OLEK: What?

WITEK: Shoes.

OLEK: Shoes?

WITEK: Shoes. Maciek said people here only look at two things: the shoes and the teeth.

OLEK: Yeah, you're right. He's got nice shoes. Maybe I can borrow them when I go to Zosia's tonight.

WITEK: Why do you think he did it?

OLEK: This Mexican?

WITEK: He's not Mexican.

OLEK: I know...Maybe his feet were hurting him. Once my feet hurt me so bad, I would have done anything to get off them.

WITEK: Oh , shut up. You know. If we don't paint the whole apartment we won't get paid.

OLEK: I know. I know. I know. Fuck it. There's no fucking justice in this world.

WITEK: I know.

OLEK: I know, I've got it.

WITEK: What?

OLEK: I'll search his pockets.

WITEK: Don't do it.

OLEK: [*Gets down on his knees, crosses himself, gets up and starts searching the dead man's pockets.*] This is the duty of any one who finds a hanging man. I heard about a man who hanged himself with $5,000 dollars in his pocket... that's not him... [*Sadly.*] One works hard, one gives his whole heart away to his painting job, and this asshole has the right to just walk in here and hang himself. Free fucking country.

WITEK: Shut up. Let me think.

OLEK: In Zelazowa Wola, if someone felt like hanging himself he would go home quietly, would put the rope around his neck, kick the chair and that's it! This is what you have a home for.

WITEK: [*Reflecting.*] You know, Olek, renovating is like fucking a tiger. A lot of fun, but scary.

OLEK: You really fucked a tiger?

WITEK: I'm just speaking metaphorically. Jesus Christ, do I have to explain everything to you? Sometimes talking to you makes me want to hang myself, too.

OLEK: Don't do it. Look. [*He opens and closes his hands into fists.*]

WITEK: So what ?

OLEK: [*Pointing to the body.*] He can't do it.

[*Noises offstage.*]

OLEK: I don't get why that fucking playwright doesn't just go back to Poland.

WITEK: Actually, I heard his grandmother on his ex-wife's side was half Jewish.

OLEK: [*Understanding.*] Ahhh... Poor bastard... So, this is why he's screwed. I can't believe it. [OLEK *grabs a bucket and his paints and ignoring the corpse, enters another room.*]

WITEK: What do you think you're doing?

OLEK: [*Offstage.*] I'm painting. I'm a working man, I won't let any hanging man disturb me.

WITEK: So how are you going to paint the ceiling? He will be covered with paint.

OLEK: [*Reenters.*] I've got it. Let's take him down, put him in the room we've already painted, and afterwards hang him back again. That way, everybody will think he hanged himself after we painted.

WITEK: Are you crazy? You are supposed to be Catholic.

OLEK: You're right. The police could find out. Better not touch the body.

[*Enter* PLAYWRIGHT: *tired, dirty, with paint all over his clothes and body. He's carrying a thick copy of* The New York Times *under his arm. He does not notice the hanging body.*]

WITEK: [*Pointing at the* PLAYWRIGHT.] Look!

OLEK: What? You don't like him, but he's brilliant. I always say that one should hang out with people on certain level. He got the solution.

WITEK: You don't like him. But he's a good playwright. He's already got a solution.

OLEK: What?

WITEK: Of course. We'll cover him [*Points to the hanging body.*] with the *Times*, then paint the ceiling, then take the paper off and we'll be done. [*Reaches his hand out to the playwright.*] Give it to me.

PLAYWRIGHT: [*Slightly confused.*] It has the Home section. [*He then notices the body and stares with a stoned look on his face.*] Oh my God. He's got nice shoes.

[*Chopin's "Grand Polonaise in A Flat" is heard.*]

WITEK: What's that?

[*Everybody listens to the music in silence.*]

OLEK: Chopin's "Grand Polonaise in A Flat." I'm playing.

BLACKOUT

THE END

David Ives

DEGAS, C'EST MOI

DAVID IVES

David Ives was born in Chicago and educated at Northwestern University and Yale School of Drama. A 1995 Guggenheim Fellow in playwriting, he is probably best known for *All In the Timing* an evening of one-act comedies first produced by Primary Stages in New York and subsequently in Chicago, San Francisco, Seattle, Dallas, Philadelphia, Washington, St. Louis, Berlin, Vienna, and Sydney, among many other places here and abroad. *All In The Timing* was awarded an Outer Critics Circle Award for playwriting, was nominated for a Drama Desk Award for best play, was included in *The Best Short Plays of 1993–94*, and was the most-performed play nationally (except for Shakespeare productions) in the 1995–96 season. Other plays by David Ives include: *Don Juan In Chicago*; *Ancient History*; *The Land of Cockaigne*; the short plays *English Made Simple*; *Seven Menus*; *Foreplay or the Art of the Fugue*; *Mere Mortals*; *Long Ago and Far Away*; and an opera, *The Secret Garden*, which premiered at the Pennsylvania Opera Theatre. Two other of his short plays, *Sure Thing* and *The Universal Language*, have been included in the *Best Short Plays* series.

This play is for Martha, of course.

SETTING: ED, *on a bed. Morning light. A grey wall behind him.*

ED: I decide to be Degas for a day. Edgar Degas. Why Degas? Why not Degas? Pourquoi pas Degas? Maybe it's the creamy white light spreading on my walls this morning...

[*Creamy white light spreads on the wall.*]

Maybe it's the prismatic bars of color on the ceiling...

[*Prismatic bars appear at the top of the wall.*]

Maybe it's all the cheap French wine I've been drinking... [*He finds a wine bottle in his bed.*] But yes, today I will be Degas! It's true, I don't know much about Degas.

[*SLIDE: Degas is projected on the wall.*]

Dead, French, impressionist painter of ballerinas...

[*SLIDE: A Degas dance scene.*]

... jockeys...

[*SLIDE: A Degas racetrack scene.*]

... and ummm...

[*SLIDE: Nothing.*]

... that kind of thing. And granted, I'm not French, dead, or a painter of any kind. And yet—are Edgar Degas and I not united by our shared humanity?

[*SLIDE of Degas, again.*]

By our common need for love?

[*SLIDE: Doisneau's photo, "The Kiss."*]

Coffee?

[*SLIDE: A cup of coffee.*]

Deodorant?

[*SLIDE: A naked armpit that disappears as DORIS enters.*]

DORIS: Oh God, oh God, oh God. Have you seen my glasses?

ED: Doris breaks in on my speculations.

DORIS: I can't find my glasses.

ED: Doris, I say to Doris, I'm going to be Degas today.

DORIS: He's gonna kill me if I'm late again.

ED: Doris doesn't see the brilliance of the idea.

DORIS: This is a tragedy.

ED: Doris—I am Degas!

DORIS: Don't forget the dry cleaning.

[DORIS *kisses him, and exits.*]

ED: Alas, poor Doris. Distracted by the banal, as usual. No matter. I start my day and brush my teeth as Degas.

[ED *hops out of bed and produces a green toothbrush. The bed disappears.*]

Wow! This is wonderful! In the bathroom, everything seems different, yet nothing has changed. The very sink seems transfigured. The porcelain pullulates with possibilities. And will you look at the light on that green plastic! The bristles are disgusting, but the light is fantastic!

[*We hear the sound of shower running.*]

In the shower, it feels strange, lathering an immortal. What's even stranger, the immortal is lathering back. How did I become such a genius? I, who flunked wood shop in high school? Was it my traumatic childhood?

[*SLIDE: A boy of five.*]

My lost pencil box?

[*SLIDE: A pencil box, marked, "Lost Pencil Box."*]

Uncle Stosh's unfortunate party trick with the parakeet?

[*SLIDE: A Parakeet.*]

That parakeet helped make me what I am. I'm great. I'm brilliant. My name will live forever! [*He considers that a second.*] No. It's too big. Too big. And I'm hungry.

[*SLIDE: Two fried eggs. Sound of frying.* ED *shakes a frying pan.*]

Frying my eggs I get fascinated by the lustrous yellow of the yolks, the burnt sienna around the edges... Something burning? My muffin. [*Produces a completely blackened muffin.*] Being Degas is going to take some practice. [*Tosses the muffin away.*] I go out into the world with dry cleaning.

[*He grabs some clothing as we hear city noises, cars honking, etc. The light changes and a SLIDE of a city skyline appears.*]

O glorious polychromatic city, saturated with light! Gone the dreary daily deja vu. Today—Degas vu.

[*A* CAR DRIVER *enters at a run, holding a steering wheel, headed right for* ED. *Loud car horn and screeching brakes heard as* ED *dodges aside.*]

ED: Idiot!

DRIVER: Moron! Watch where you're going!

ED: Jerk! Do you know who you almost killed?

DRIVER: Asshole!

[DRIVER *exits.*]

ED: Another couple of inches and the world would've lost a hundred masterpieces.

[DRY CLEANER *enters, writing on a pad.*]

DRY CLEANER: What can I do for you, honey?

ED: At the dry cleaners I notice something strange...

DRY CLEANER: [*Taking the dry cleaning.*] One shirt, one skirt, one jacket.

ED: My dry cleaner acts exactly the same.

DRY CLEANER: You know you need some serious reweaving.

ED: Madame, I would love to capture you in charcoal.

DRY CLEANER: My husband already caught me in puce. [*Tears a sheet off the pad.*] After five. [THE DRY CLEANER *gives the slip to* ED, *and exits with the clothing.*]

ED: Not a flutter. Then, on the corner, the newsguy tries to sell me my paper just like always.

[NEWSGUY *enters.*]

NEWSGUY: Daily Noose?

ED: Have you got anything en Francaise?

NEWSGUY: Let's see, I got *Le Mot, Le Monde, Le Reve, Le Chat, La Chasse, Le Mystere, Les Mamelles,* and the *Nouvel Observateur.*

ED: I'll take the *News.*

NEWSGUY: Change.

[He flips an invisible coin, which ED *"catches," then the* NEWSGUY *exits.]*

ED: Still not a blink of recognition. Then as I head down Broadway, people pass me by without a second glance. Or a third, or a fourth.

*[*PEOPLE *enter and pass him.]*

I might as well be invisible. I, Edgar Degas!

[More PEOPLE *pass him.]*

And then I realize with a shock: it makes no difference to be Degas. I could be anyone!

[More PEOPLE *pass him.]*

And yet... And yet maybe the other Degas walked this invisibly through Paris.

[SLIDE: A Degas street scene of Paris, as we hear a French accordion and the clip-clopping of horses.]

Bumped into by the bourgeoisie on the upper Left Bank...

[A PEDESTRIAN *bumps into him as a* WORKER *enters carrying a crate loaded with cabbages.]*

Shouted at by workers at the Key Food de Montparnasse...

WORKER: Watcha back, watcha back!

*[*WORKER *exits.]*

ED: Cursed by the less fortunate.

*[*HOMELESS PERSON *enters.]*

HOMELESS PERSON: Fuck you. Fuck you.

ED: There's a kind of comfort in this.

HOMELESS PERSON: Fuck you.

ED: Completely anonymous, I'm free to appreciate the grey blur of pigeons...

[*SLIDE: Flying pigeons.*]

The impasto at Ray's Pizza ...

[*SLIDE: Pizza window.*]

The chiaroscuro of the M-11 bus.

[*SLIDE: A city bus. An* UNEMPLOYMENT WORKER *enters.*]

UNEMPLOYMENT WORKER: Next!

ED: My delicious anonymity continues at Unemployment.

[*Accordion and horses stop as a sign descends which says, "Line Forms Here."*]

UNEMPLOYMENT WORKER: Sign your claim at the bottom, please.

ED: Do you notice the name I signed in the bottom right corner?

UNEMPLOYMENT WORKER: Edgar Day-hass. Edgar Deejis. Edgar Deggis. Edgar De Gas. Edgar De What?

ED: Edgar Degas. And—?

UNEMPLOYMENT WORKER: And—this name at the bottom does not match the name at the top of the form.

ED: No, no, no, no ...

UNEMPLOYMENT WORKER: Are you not the same as the person at the top of the form?

ED: I am a person at the top of my form. I am Edgar. Degas.

UNEMPLOYMENT WORKER: The dead French painter?

ED: The same.

UNEMPLOYMENT WORKER: Next!

[UNEMPLOYMENT WORKER *exits and the sign goes away.*]

ED: Recalling my painterly interest in racetracks, I stop off at OTB.

[*SLIDE: A Degas Racetrack scene, as another sign descends which also says, "Line Forms Here."* OTB WORKER *enters.*]

OTB WORKER: Next!

ED: I would like to put ten francs on Windmill.

OTB WORKER: Oh mais oui, monsieur.

ED: Windmill—I say to him—because the jockey wears brilliant silks of crimson and gold. Windmill—I tell the man—because her sable flanks flash like lightning in the field.

OTB WORKER: [*Handing over the betting slip.*] Windmill—

ED: —he says to me—

OTB WORKER:—always comes in last.

ED: And Windmill does. But who cares? [*Tears up the betting slip.*] I'm Degas!

[OTB WORKER *exits and the sign goes away. SLIDE: the City Library.*]

Oh. The library. Maybe I should look myself up.

[*A Sign descends: "Silence." A* LIBRARIAN *enters.*]

Excuse me. Have you got anything on Degas?

LIBRARIAN: The crassly conservative counterfeminist patriarchal pedophile painter?

ED: No, the colorist who chronicled his age and continues to inspire through posters, postcards and T-shirts.

LIBRARIAN: Section D, aisle 2.

[LIBRARIAN *exits.*]

ED: Who needs the carping of critics, the lies of biographers? I know who I am. Famished by creativity, I stop at Twin Donut.

[*SLIDE: A donut, as two tables appear. A* YOUNG WOMAN *sits at one, writing in a journal.* ED *sits at the other.*]

TWIN DONUT WORKER: [*Enters with a plate.*] Vanilla cruller?

ED: Ici! And some drawing paper, please.

[DONUT WORKER *hands him a napkin.*]

ED: [*Cont'd.*] There I am, scribbling a priceless doodle on my napkin when I notice someone staring at me.

[*The* YOUNG WOMAN *stops writing and, pausing for thought, looks at* ED.]

ED: [*Cont'd.*] A young woman writing in a journal. Has she recognized me? She smiles slightly. Yes. She knows I am Degas. Not only that. [*He looks again.*] She loves Degas. That one look has redeemed all my years of effort. My work has given meaning to someone's life. Should I seduce her? It would be traditional.

[*A schmaltzy-romantic violin is heard.*]

YOUNG WOMAN: [*Writing.*] "April six. Twin Donut. Just saw Edgar Degas two tables over. So he likes vanilla crullers too! Suddenly this day is glorious and memorable. Would love to lie in bed all afternoon and make love with Degas... "

ED: But no. I'd only cast her off, break her heart. Not to mention what it would do to Doris.

YOUNG WOMAN: "Dwayne would kill me."

ED: But isn't it my duty as an artist to seduce this girl? Experience life to the fullest...?

YOUNG WOMAN: Adieu.

ED: Adieu.

[YOUNG WOMAN *exits and the tables disappear. Afternoon light. Street sounds and a SLIDE of a city street again.*]

ED: On Fifth Avenue, a mysterious figure passes me, leading a Doberman. Or vice versa.

[*A* FIGURE *in a raincoat, hat and sunglasses, holding a stiffened leash, as if a dog were on it, crosses.*]

ED: [*Cont'd.*] Somebody famous. But who? Woody Allen? Kissinger? Roseanne? Then other things distract me. Money...

[*SLIDE: A dollar bill.*]

Job...

[*SLIDE: The want ads.*]

Athlete's foot...

[*SLIDE: A naked foot.*]

But wait a minute. Whoa, whoa, whoa! For a picosecond there, I forgot: I am Degas!

[*SLIDE: Photo of Degas. A* HOT DOG VENDOR *enters.*]

HOT DOG VENDOR: Hot dog! Hot dog! Hot dog!

ED: The labor of hanging onto one's identity amidst the daily dreck.

HOT DOG VENDOR: You got a pretzel here!

ED: It's too much.

HOT DOG VENDOR: Good Humor! Good Humor!

[*Empty picture frames descend, as the* VENDOR *exits and a* MU-SEUM GUARD *enters.*]

ED: At the museum, I tour the rooms of my work. Amazing how much I accomplished—even without television.

[*SLIDE: A Degas self-portrait.*]

A self-portrait. Not a great likeness, maybe. But so full of...what?...feeling. I stare into my fathomless eyes.

[*A* MUSEUMGOER *enters and stands beside him looking at the self-portrait.*]

MUSEUMGOER: Mmm.

ED: Mmmmmmmm.

MUSEUMGOER: Bit smudgy, isn't it?

ED: "Smudgy?"

MUSEUMGOER: This area in here.

ED: Yeah, but what about this area over here?

MUSEUMGOER: No, but this area here. Something not quite realized.

ED: Okay. So I had an off day.

MUSEUMGOER: Off day?

ED: Not all my work was perfect.

MUSEUMGOER: Indeed. Indeed...

[THE MUSEUMGOER *slips away.*]

ED: Philistine. Probably headed for Van Gogh. To kneel in adoration at the sunflowers—of course. Vincent. "Vince," we called him. What a jerk.

[*SLIDE: "Woman with Chrysanthemums."*]

What's this..."Woman with Chrysanthemums." Ah, yes. A personal favorite. God, when I remember that morning over a century ago—can it be that long now?—when this was an empty canvas and I stood in front it paralyzed by its whiteness. Then I reached for my brush ... [*He produces a paintbrush.*] ... and it all crystallized. I saw it all. This pensive woman, oblivious of the transcendent burst of color right at her shoulder. The natural exuberance of the flowers—alongside her human sorrow. Yes. Yes! Our blindness to the beautiful! Our insensibility to the splendor right there within our reach! When I finished, I was exalted. Will I ever have a day that inspired again ... ?

MUSEUM GUARD: Step back, please.

ED: Excuse me?

MUSEUM GUARD: You have to step back, sir. You're too close to the painting.

ED: I'm too close to this painting ... ?

MUSEUM GUARD: Do you copy?

ED: No, I don't copy.

MUSEUM GUARD: Sir?

ED: I step back.

[*He does so, and the SLIDE fades out and the picture frames fly up out of sight. The GUARD exits.*]

But the glow of my exaltation stays with me all the way to the Akropolis Diner ...

[*Two tables again. DORIS enters.*]

DORIS: Oh God, oh God, oh God.

ED: ... where Doris meets me for dinner.

DORIS: What a day.

ED: What a fabulous day. Epic!

DORIS: Six hours of xeroxing.

ED: No, but listen. Degas. Remember?

DORIS: Degas ... ?

ED: I've been Degas all day. Since morning.

DORIS: The toilets erupted again. The women's room was like Vesuvius.

ED: I am Degas.

[WAITER *enters.*]

WAITER: What do you need, my friends?

ED: Cherie?

DORIS: Alka Seltzer.

WAITER: One Bromo.

DORIS: Make it a double.

WAITER: And you, sir?

ED: I'll have a Reubens.

WAITER: We got a Rube! [*Exits.*]

DORIS: They said they were going to fix those toilets last week.

ED: As Doris dilates on toilets, I begin to feel Degas slip away a little...

DORIS: Waiter!

ED: ...like a second skin I'm shedding...

DORIS: Waiter!

ED: ... leaving nothing behind.

DORIS: Where is that guy?

ED: Then I see a man at another table, staring at me. Looking at me with such pity in his eyes. Such unalloyed human sympathy.

DORIS: At least I found my glasses.

ED: Then I realize.

DORIS: They were in my purse all the time.

ED: The man is Renoir.

DORIS: [*Holding up her glasses.*] See?

ED: By now, Degas is completely gone.

[*Light changes to night light, the rear wall darkens to black, as* ED *and* DORIS *rise from the tables, and the tables disappear.*]

ED: [*Cont'd.*] Doris and I walk home in silence.

[DORIS *exits.* ED *is alone, as the lights darken further around him, to a single spot.*]

ED: [*Cont'd.*] People say they have a voice inside their heads. The voice that tells themselves the story of their lives. Now I'm walking up the street, now I'm taking out my key, is there a meaning to all this, who's that person on the stairway coming down, now I'm putting my key in the door, now I do this, now I do that. The facts of our lives. Yes, I too have always had a voice like that in my head. But now, tonight, no one is listening. That presence that always listened in the back of my mind is no longer there, listening in. Nor is there a presence behind that presence listening in. Nor a presence behind that, nor behind that, nor behind that. All the way back to the back of my mind, no one is listening in. The story of my life is going on unwatched. Unheard. I am alone.

[*The bed reappears.* ED *sprawls on it, his forearm over his eyes.*]

I find myself upstairs, sprawled on the bed while Doris runs the bathwater. Degas is dust. All my glory, all my fame, all my achievements are utterly forgotten. Immortality? A cruel joke. I have done nothing. Absolutely nothing...

[*A light comes up on* DORIS, *drying herself with a towel.*]

Then I find myself looking through the doorway into the bathroom and I see Doris standing naked with her foot up on the edge of the old lion-footed tub, drying herself. The overhead light is dim, but Doris is fluorescent—radiant—luminous—with pinks and lavenders and vermillions playing over her skin. The frayed towel she's wrapped in gleams like a rose. She turns and looks back at me and smiles.

[DORIS *turns and looks over her shoulder at* ED.]

DORIS: Bon soir, Degas.

ED: Degas? Who needs him?

[*He holds his hand out to her across the intervening space, and she holds hers out to him.*]

Lights fade

THE END

Allan Knee

THE ST. VALENTINE'S DAY MASSACRE

ALLAN KNEE

Allan Knee wrote the award-winning adaptation of *Around the World In Eighty Days*, which was chosen last summer by Theaterworks/USA for New York City's free summer theater. His other plays include *Shmulnik's Waltz* (Jewish Rep), *The Lost Boys* (American Repertory Theater, Cambridge), *Second Avenue* (Manhattan Puchline), *The Minister's Black Veil* (Playwright's Horizons), *Santa Anita '42* (Chelsea Theater at the Brooklyn Academy of Music), and the Broadway musical, *Late Nite Comic*. His one-act play, *Christmas Eve On Orchard Street*, was included in *Best American Short Plays of 1990*. For television he wrote the four-part PBS series of Nathaniel Hawthorne's *The Scarlett Letter* and *A Gorey Halloween*, based on the characters of Edward Gorey. His film, *Journey*, won a Cine Eagle at the Washington Film Festival. His current projects include a musical adaptation of *Little Women* (with Alison Hubbard and Kim Oler) and an original musical *Dancing On The Rooftops* (with Jon Marans and Daniel Levine). He is a graduate of the Yale School of Drama.

SETTING: *A cafe in some part of town. February 14. A man and a woman in their early 30s confront one another. The man, KENNY, is enthusiastic as he takes off his coat, sets down a package. The woman, SHERYL, stylish, is more wary. They are both in an emotional, edgy state.*

KENNY: Sheryl, I almost didn't recognize you. You look so—

SHERYL: Terrific?

KENNY: Yes! I can't get over it. The ensemble. The suit, the hair. You've got such—

SHERYL: Style?

KENNY: Style! Yes! This must have been a fantastic year for you. My God, no more fatigue boots—no more army surplus!

SHERYL: Well, look at you. No more pin-striped suits? wing-tipped shoes?

KENNY: Don't be fooled by appearances. This is a very, very studied look. [*Holding out his arm.*] Feel this. Go on—feel it.

SHERYL: I'm really not interested in your body.

KENNY: Feel it, Sheryl.

[*She feels his leg with a finger—makes a sour face*]

KENNY: [*Cont'd.*] My personal trainer is very enthusiastic about my progress.

SHERYL: You have a personal trainer?

KENNY: Actually, I have two—one for the upper part of the body— one for the lower.

SHERYL: I can only stay 15 minutes. I can't waste a whole afternoon.

KENNY: You're not still pissed at me, are you? Surely, you've forgiven me?

SHERYL: For being an asshole? Yes, I've forgiven you for that.

KENNY: Good. I've forgiven you, too.

SHERYL: What have you forgiven me for?

KENNY: Let's see. Lack of insight—peevishness—small mindedness—

SHERYL: I'm going. [*She gets up.*]

KENNY: [*Stopping her.*] It's a joke! I admit there were misunderstandings! And, more than once, I was a little bit at fault.

SHERYL: A little bit?

KENNY: I'm not perfect. But you have to admit I'm pretty close to it. Now, sit down. Please. Finish your drink at least.

[*She sits back down.*]

KENNY: [*Cont'd.*] What we're doing I think Valentine himself would have been proud of. It's clearly something he would have done if he had had the opportunity. And maybe he did, who knows—maybe he met his girl over drinks, overlooking the park. Valentine was a great sentimentalist.

SHERYL: Like you.

KENNY: I don't mind the comparison. In fact, I rather like it. Shall I tell you about St. Valentine?

SHERYL: Let me see if I remember what you told me last year. He was misunderstood by the church, ill-treated by his peers, abused by his parents, and martyred by society.

KENNY: And why? Why I ask you? Why did this misfortune happen?

SHERYL: Because he was an unfaithful, irresponsbile bastard!

KENNY: No, Sheryl, you're wrong again. If Valentine had any failings—it was being too faithful. Too caring. He loved too much.

SHERYL: They martyr people for loving too much?

KENNY: That is the number one cause of martyrdom in the Western world. Read your church history. The good die young. Listen to your Billy Joel. Cruel, nasty men live long lives and die peacefully in their sleep. The good suffer ignominies, premature baldness, constipation, IRS audits, and wet dreams. Say what you want about me, Sheryl, but don't mock Valentine. He was a defender of the faith. He died for love. And no one dies for love anymore. I get the feeling you don't believe in love anymore, either.

SHERYL: Not really.

KENNY: Something sour you on it?

SHERYL: Someone.

KENNY: Present company excluded of course?

SHERYL: Kenny, can we stop this crap right now? When I agreed to meet with you once a year, I agreed to it because I thought it'd be fun—quirky, perhaps—at least somehow it'd be interesting. But, it hasn't been interesting, it's not been quirky, and it's never been fun.

KENNY: Well, not for you maybe, but I've had a hell of a good time.

SHERYL: I'm sick and tired of warring with you.

KENNY: Then I surrender.

SHERYL: No, you don't surrender. You have to win all the time.

KENNY: Everyone likes a little victory. Don't you?

SHERYL: I'm not about winning or losing. I've changed.

KENNY: Obviously. You reek of confidence now—you have an aura of magnificence about you. The clothes, the hair. You exude the odor of the first floor of Bloomingdale's. So, talk to me. Tell me what's going on.

SHERYL: I went to a psychic.

KENNY: [Surprised.] You went to a fortune teller?

SHERYL: No, Kenny, I went to a psychic—who advised me to stop seeing you.

KENNY: But you don't see me.

SHERYL: [Mounting anger.] For three years, six months, and four days I saw you. We lived together for more than two of those years. We shared the same bathroom, Kenny. I gave you the best three years of my life.

KENNY: And you want them back now?

SHERYL: Yes! Yes, I do! Can you give them back to me?

KENNY: I'm not holding on to them.

SHERYL: Bullshit!

KENNY: Maybe a few memories.

SHERYL: Rupert advised me to reverse everything I was doing.

KENNY: Rupert?

SHERYL: The pyschic. He advised me to make a long list of my activities—the things I did, the places I went, my behavioral patterns. So I did. I voted Republican. I started eating meat. I changed my way of dressing. And I took a job with Drexel Burnham.

KENNY: The brokerage house? I thought they were all behind bars—or living in Argentina.

SHERYL: They started up again.

KENNY: Incredible.

SHERYL: They're just the ones that got caught, that's all.

KENNY: Oh, so they're more to be pitied than censured? You're endorsing dishonesty, Sheryl.

SHERYL: It's the way of the world.

KENNY: And you've jumped on the bandwagon? Congratulations. What do you do at Drexel?

SHERYL: I'm a stockbroker.

KENNY: [Cries out.] I don't believe it! A stockbroker? Tell me you turn the switch on the electric chair, but don't tell me you sell stocks! What happened to your passion for the people?

SHERYL: [Bites out.] It died! Like a lot of things die! You give up you go on! You see the futility of things! I'm a stockbroker! And a good one! You don't like it? Tough shit!

KENNY: Forgive me. I'm just so happy to see you.

SHERYL: This is how you express your happiness?

KENNY: Your skin looks terrific. Like crystal.

SHERYL: I had a chemical peel.

KENNY: That must have taken real guts.

SHERYL: The skin's still a little raw.

KENNY: Looks great. Sheryl, did you know that birds pick their life-long mates on St. Valentine's Day?

SHERYL: How do they know it's St. Valentine's Day?

KENNY: They check with Audubon—I don't know. Instinct, perhaps. So, you're a stockbroker?

SHERYL: Yes.

KENNY: Happy?

SHERYL: Most of the time.

KENNY: Making money?

SHERYL: Enough.

KENNY: Getting laid? Forget that question. [*He laughs nervously, stops.*] Are you getting laid? You look so sexually satisfied.

SHERYL: I am.

KENNY: You're not being promiscuous, I hope?

SHERYL: Kenny, you look tired, old and worn. You're spending your days at the gym trying to change your body image. But, unfortunately, you're still a very shabby, flabby man!

KENNY: God, I miss you. I miss someone who could talk to me like that. Put me in my place—smack me around—

SHERYL: I never smacked you. Though often enough I wanted to.

KENNY: Would you like to smack me, now? You can, you know. Give me a good old-fashioned smack. Go on, Sheryl. Let me have it.

[*She smacks him—surprisingly hard.*]

KENNY: [*Cont'd.*] You obviously still love me.

SHERYL: I'm over you, Kenny.

KENNY: So, why did you come today?

SHERYL: To tell you I've met someone.

KENNY: Someone you like?

SHERYL: Enormously.

KENNY: Is it a man?

SHERYL: Yes.

KENNY: You're sleeping with him?

SHERYL: This is 1995, Kenny.

KENNY: So, you're not sleeping with him?

SHERYL: I've got to be going.

KENNY: [*Calls.*] You want to handle my account?

SHERYL: No.

KENNY: Sheryl—

SHERYL: Go elsewhere. Go to Merrill Lynch.

KENNY: I hate Merrill Lynch. What's he look like?

SHERYL: Who?

KENNY: Your boyfriend.

SHERYL: A cross between Al Pacino and Mel Gibson.

KENNY: That short, huh? I hope he's wealthy.

SHERYL: Millions.

KENNY: I'm sure he's conservative?

SHERYL: Democrat.

KENNY: Virile?

SHERYL: He shaves twice a day.

KENNY: Romantic?

SHERYL: Kenny, go find some 18-year-old co-ed who still believes in St. Valentine's Day—because I don't! And I think we should stop this!

KENNY: Stop what?

SHERYL: Meeting. Year after year. It's getting us nowhere.

KENNY: We were once lovers! When your father died I held you in my arms for a week—

SHERYL: People break up all the time and that's the end of it. They don't set up meetings once a year to carry on some inane tradition.

KENNY: Inane? This is the most important day of the year for me! I was like a child waking up this morning! "Valentine's Day!" I cried out. "It's Valentine's Day!" I danced out of bed!

SHERYL: Don't you get it, Kenny—I don't love you anymore? I'm not interested in you. You're just a man with a lot of worn-out opinions.

KENNY: [*He goes to her and puts his hands affectionately on hers. His voice soft and intimate.*] I hate myself.

SHERYL: Please, stop this.

KENNY: I look in the mirror every morning and think what an ugly bastard I am.

SHERYL: Please take your hands off of me.

KENNY: I can't.

SHERYL: Kenny, please—

KENNY: They seem to be stuck to you. Must be some sort of chemical acid on your clothes.

SHERYL: [*Pulling away.*] I'm not amused.

KENNY: Sheryl, I have a confession.

SHERYL: What is it?

KENNY: "I get no kick from champagne, mere alcohol—"

SHERYL: Stop it—please stop it.

KENNY: Are you really seeing someone?

SHERYL: I told you I was.

KENNY: Where'd you meet him?

SHERYL: At Drexel.

KENNY: He's a broker?

SHERYL: A client.

KENNY: You're fucking a client?

SHERYL: Yes.

KENNY: Isn't that unethical?

SHERYL: Not in the brokerage business! [*She starts to leave.*] Have a wonderful life, Kenny. Nice seeing you again.

KENNY: [*Calls desperately.*] Sheryl—I'm dying!

SHERYL: [*Turns, stunned.*] What?

KENNY: I didn't want to tell you.

SHERYL: You're dying?

KENNY: That's why I look so lousy.

SHERYL: Don't kid about something like this.

KENNY: I'm not kidding.

SHERYL: What are you dying of?

KENNY: I don't want to upset you.

SHERYL: Is it AIDS?

KENNY: Worse.

SHERYL: What?

KENNY: Diaper rash. An advanced case.

SHERYL: Goddam you, you make fun of everything!

KENNY: Itch all night—

SHERYL: Nothing is sacred to you.

KENNY: [*Strong.*] Everything is sacred to me! Life is sacred to me! Love is sacred to me! You are sacred to me! St. Valentine is sacred to me!

SHERYL: St. Valentine is a made-up saint!

KENNY: A made-up saint? Says who?

SHERYL: Says everyone. He's a fraud—like you.

KENNY: I'm a fraud, am I?

SHERYL: Face up to it, Kenny! We don't mix well. We're like oil and water. It doesn't work for us!

KENNY: Because you're a stubborn, spoiled, inhibited bitch.

SHERYL: I am not inhibited! I may be spoiled—I may be stubborn at times—but I have a very alive body!

KENNY: Miss Frigidaire!

SHERYL: That is amusing—that is really amusing, Kenny, coming from a 34-year-old, adolescent boy scout whose idea of being kinky is making love in his shredded underwear!

KENNY: You found my shredded underwear irresistible.

SHERYL: The truth is, I found your shredded Fruit-Of-The-Looms® disgusting.

KENNY: You said I reminded you of Tom Cruise.

SHERYL: And I hate Tom Cruise!

KENNY: You said *Born On The 4th of July* was your favorite movie.

SHERYL: I lied! I found it indulgent and tiresome! I don't want this anymore! I stopped wanting this four years ago! I can still see you crawling in bed with me in your long johns and smelly socks, reading your dirty little books—your how-to manuals—setting out like some demented sex therapist to find my G-spot, when all I wanted from you was some genuine passion. I wanted to lose myself in you. I wanted wild, filthy conversation.

KENNY: You wanted me to talk dirty to you?

SHERYL: Yes!

KENNY: This is amazing! This is really amazing, Sheryl! It's what I wanted to do! I wanted to talk filth to you! I used to fantasize about you constantly, everywhere. Once, at a Passover seder, I imagined I was Elijah and entered the room wrapped only in a sheet, and while everyone was blessing the matzoh, I took you on the table before my folks, my cousins, my aunts. Talk about passion, filth, blasphemy!

SHERYL: Kenny, please!

KENNY: I couldn't go to a museum without imagining every nude was you—

SHERYL: Stop!

KENNY: I'd ravish you—

SHERYL: Kenny!

KENNY: And, I wouldn't let up even if you shouted—

SHERYL: Enough!

KENNY: I'd keep at it! I'd come at you again and again.

SHERYL: This is madness.

KENNY: Wild, vile words would pour out of me. And I'd stand over you like a collosus with my penis unsheathed and I'd howl—

SHERYL: Stop.

KENNY: —and make all sorts of noises while you'd be screaming—

SHERYL: Give it to me hard!

KENNY: Yes!

SHERYL: Ravish me!

KENNY: Bite me!

SHERYL: Hurt me!

KENNY: Yes!

SHERYL: Screw me!

KENNY: Oh, God, yes!

SHERYL: Don't stop!

KENNY: No!

SHERYL: Kenny!

KENNY: I'd do it eight—nine times in a night!

SHERYL: More!

KENNY: Tigers do it 16 times in a three-hour span!

SHERYL: Oh, my tiger!

KENNY: [*Growls.*] My Sheryl.

SHERYL: Kenny!

KENNY: Sheryl!

SHERYL: Kenny!

KENNY: Sheryllll!

SHERYL: [*Overlapping.*] Kenneeee!

[*They both cry out in ecstasy. Gradually, they come to themselves, embarrassed.* SHERYL *straightens herself.*]

SHERYL: [*Cont'd.*] I've got to go.

KENNY: I know. It's late for me, too. I'll pay the check.

SHERYL: You can't afford it.

KENNY: I can afford it.

SHERYL: Look, let's not stand on ceremonies. If you're broke—

KENNY: I'm not broke.

SHERYL: You're obviously out of work.

KENNY: Who said I'm out of work?

SHERYL: You said—

KENNY: I've got a job with a law firm.

SHERYL: As what?

KENNY: A lawyer.

SHERYL: Bullshit! A lawyer? Since when?

KENNY: Last June.

SHERYL: You finally passed the bar? I don't believe it.

KENNY: Third time lucky.

SHERYL: But the clothes?

KENNY: It's dress-down day at the company.

SHERYL: Dress-down? You're kidding?

KENNY: No.

SHERYL: We tried it at Drexel, dressing down—the clients went crazy. They thought the bottom was falling out of the market.

KENNY: It takes a little getting used to. But people come around.

SHERYL: Do they?

KENNY: You know what? Getting together with you—once a year, one day a year, a few hours, a few minutes even—is the sanest thing I do.

SHERYL: [*She gets up.*] I've really got to go now.

[*When she hesitates,* KENNY *suddenly senses he could have her back, but all he says is:*]

KENNY: Me too...

SHERYL: [*She stops, looks at him.*] Next year I pick the place.

KENNY: You really getting married?

SHERYL: I'm thinking of it.

KENNY: No matter what—this day is ours.

SHERYL: The last two devotees of St. Valentine. [*She starts away again.*]

KENNY: [*Calls.*] Sheryl?

SHERYL: Yes?

KENNY: I love you.

SHERYL: You really fantasized all that about me?

KENNY: I still do. I wish—

SHERYL: [*Stopping him.*] Kenny, please. Bye.

KENNY: Bye.

[*They do not move.*]

THE END

Jonathan Levy

OLD BLUES

For Mary

JONATHAN LEVY

Jonathan Levy received his B.A. from Harvard University, and his M.A. and Ph.D. from Columbia University. He has had over thirty plays and libretti for adults and children produced at the Brooklyn Academy of Music, Alice Tully Hall, Phoenix Theatre, Manhattan Theatre Club, American Shakespeare Festival in Stratford, Connecticutt, the Eugene O'Neill Playwrights Conference, and Playwrights Horizons, to name a few. His play *Charlie The Chicken* was included in *The Best Short Plays of 1983*.

From 1973 through 1978, he was the playwright in residence at the Manhattan Theatre Club, and then acted as their Literary Advisor from 1982 through 1984. He was a member of the National Endowment for the Arts Theatre Policy Panel, and was Co-Chairman of Theatre For Youth from 1979 through 1981.

Presently, Dr. Levy is a Distinguished Teaching Professor in Education at SUNY Stony Brook, a professor in Harvard's Graduate School of Education, and a Chief Examiner in Theatre Arts for the International Baccalaureate.

In the past, he has taught at Brandeis University, Columbia College, University of California at Berkley, Bennington College, the Lincoln Center Institute, and the Juilliard School of Music, among others. In 1996 he was named Outstanding Theatre Teacher in American Higher Education by the Association for Theatre in Higher Education (ATHE).

CHARACTERS

CHRIS   Gray brush cut, gray, ravaged, boyish face. Thin, Archibald Cox bow tie. Top tenor.

EDDIE   The host. Small, enthusiastic. Lead.

BROOKS   A dandy. Styled hair. Baritone.

RICHARD   A Resident in Surgery. White hospital trousers, and a big parka, gray-green with Orlon fur, trimmed in road construction orange.

SETTING: EDDIE'S *apartment in the East sixties. Quite bare. A bar with a bowl of cheese dip and potato chips on it.*

TIME: *Winter, 1975.*

The stage is dark. Sound of a pitch pipe being blown. A throat cleared. The pitch pipe is blown again. Three voices—two tenors and a baritone—singing.

VOICES: As the blackbird in the spring
'Neath the willow tree
Sat and piped I heard him sing
Singing Aura Lee.
Aura Lee, Aura Lee,
Maid with golden hair
Sunshine came along with thee
And swallows in the air.

[*Lights up slowly on* CHRIS, EDDIE, *and* BROOKS *singing. They end. Long pause.*]

BROOKS: I thought it was pretty tactless of the minister to keep going on about Bill being convivial. Everybody knows convivial means drunk.

EDDIE: Old Billy. Son of a bitch.

BROOKS: It's going to happen to us all, and you can't ask for it quicker than Old Bill. One minute dictating behind your desk. The next, dead on the floor. [*He goes toward the kitchen.*] You want a beer, Eddie?

EDDIE: Sure.

[*Exit* BROOKS *to the kitchen.*]

EDDIE: [*Cont'd.*] Here today...

[CHRIS *walks on humming.*]

BROOKS: [*O.S.*] Where do you keep the church keys?

EDDIE: Betsy took them. Every last one we had in the house.

BROOKS: [*O.S.*] Does she collect them or what?

EDDIE: Spite. Pure spite. All the light bulbs too. You figure it. Use the can opener.

BROOKS: [*O.S.*] That's ridiculous.

EDDIE: You're telling me. I live here. [*Pause.*] You're lucky, Chris. Count yourself lucky you never got married.

[CHRIS *turns, gives him a baleful stare and walks off humming. Enter* BROOKS *with two beers.*]

BROOKS: Boy, those kids got big. That boy of his, what's his name...

CHRIS: Scott.

BROOKS: Right. Scottie. He's bigger than I am. So's the girl, for that matter...

CHRIS: Helen.

[*He walks off humming.*]

EDDIE: Why do they let them keep the coffin open? That really ticked me off. Why do they do it? It's barbaric.

BROOKS: That's the way Ann wanted it.

EDDIE: So what? Who ever listened to her before? That big red face, in with the lilies. The goddamn choir singing flat.

BROOKS: It took eight men to lift him.

EDDIE: I'm going to buried in my Whiff tie. I wrote it into the will. My Pi Eta cuff links, my Bronze Star, and my Whiff tie.

CHRIS: [*After a pause.*] I'm going to be cremated.

BROOKS: [*After a pause.*] Let's sing something.

CHRIS: [*Beginning "Mood Indigo."*]
You ain't been blue, no—oo how...

EDDIE: O God, Chris. "Mood Indigo."

[CHRIS *sings the walking bass line. It is way out of his range, but it gives some idea of how Bill sang it.*]

EDDIE: Christ, I miss him. Especially in the second chorus. He was so...

BROOKS: Convivial.

EDDIE: Companionable. That's a word, isn't it, Chris? You're the English major.

CHRIS: It's a word. It used to be a word.

[*He walks off singing "Since You Got that Mood Indigo," the walking bass line.*]

EDDIE: Listen to that. You know, when we were all singing the melody, the words, you know what Bill was singing? Bum bum bum bum. [*Pause.*] I can't help thinking he could have gotten more out of life.

CHRIS: You know what the tenor's singing when you're singing the words? [*Very high and white.*] Wah wah. Wah wah. Wah wah. [*Ad lib.*]

BROOKS: [*Under the singing.*] Who's the new guy, Eddie?

EDDIE: A nephew of old Charlie Taylor's. An ex-Whiff. Charlie says he sings up a storm. I told Charlie, what the hell, we may as well listen to him. Of course the kid is thrilled.

BROOKS: Just as a point of information, Eddie: who is old Charlie Taylor?

EDDIE: You remember. Redheaded second tenor from Hotchkiss. Took out Bob McKay's sister Junior Year.

BROOKS: Margie. The dirty blond with the bangs. God, I had the hots for that girl.

CHRIS: [*After a pause.*] Micky. Micky McKay. Short for Michele.

BROOKS: Micky McKay. What the hell ever happened to Micky McKay?

EDDIE: Probably became a nurse. She always did have good hands, right, Brooks? You ought to know.

BROOKS: [*After a pause.*] Probably a grandmother by now.

EDDIE: Right. Probably a swinging grandmother.

BROOKS: With little gray whiskers and a five handicap. And *very* cheery. I took her to the Princeton Game Senior Year. She had on a six-foot Yale scarf and one of those wooly Scotch hats with a pom-pom.

CHRIS: No you didn't.

BROOKS: What, Chris?

CHRIS: You took Nell Ellsworth. Dingo Cullen took Micky McKay.

BROOKS: Jesus, I think he's right.

CHRIS: I am right. Just don't ask me what happened last Thursday.

EDDIE: Who did I take, Chris?

CHRIS: You didn't have a date. You drank half a bottle of bourbon and puked all over the Calhoun Common.

EDDIE: What a memory.

CHRIS: Particularly since I drank the other half of the bottle.

BROOKS: What a sketch he was, that Dingo Cullen. Whipped it out at a Wellesley mixer and peed into the rhododendrons. Then he turned to all and sundry and said "When you got to go you got to go." That's the way he got the name Dingo.

CHRIS: [*After a pause.*] You're thinking of Big Dick Welles. [*Pause.*] Dingo Cullen was a microbiologist. [*Pause.*] And what he said was: "Time and tide wait for no man."

EDDIE: You know something, Chris? You were wasted as an English major. You should have been a History major.

CHRIS: [*After a pause.*] Let's sing something.

BROOKS: I'm going to get another beer.

[*He goes into the kitchen.*]

EDDIE: Hey, Brooks. Your liver doesn't care what you pour down there. Beer's as bad as booze if you drink enough of it. You keep drinking past forty, the front of your brain starts coming out through your nose.

BROOKS: [*O.S.*] Eat me, Eddie.

EDDIE: Up yours with a meathook, Brooks.

CHRIS: Boys, boys.

[CHRIS *takes out his pitch pipe and plays a note. He begins to sing.* EDDIE *joins in. Then* BROOKS *comes in from the kitchen with a beer and joins them.*]

THE THREE: Graceful and easy
I said to Mandy
Nothing is too good for you.
I said to Mandy
When she was handy
Nothing is too good for you.

EDDIE: So where is our bass?

CHRIS: "In de cold, cold ground..."

EDDIE: Don't be morbid, Chris. I meant the kid.

CHRIS: Do you know what morbid means, Eddie?

EDDIE: Tell me, Chris. You're the English major.

CHRIS: It means having to do with death. The dead. Eddie, if I didn't think continually about the dead I wouldn't have a friend in the world. [*Pause.*] Present company excepted.

BROOKS: I think that's the most I've heard Chris say at one time in ten years.

CHRIS: What's there to say.

[*He walks off, not humming. Pause.*]

EDDIE: Guess who walked into the bank the other day. Al Thomas.

BROOKS: Old Al Thomas?

EDDIE: You remember Al Thomas. Fat second bass from Indiana or Ohio or somewhere.

CHRIS: [*After a long pause.*] Terre Haute. [*He sits.*]

EDDIE: He must have made a bundle. Set up four trusts of two hundred thou apiece for his grandchildren. I tried to put him into tax-frees but he said "I'm not worried about the taxes, Eddie. Forget about the taxes. The Government has been good to me and I'm not out to screw the government."

BROOKS: I don't believe it.

EDDIE: It's true. He was something big in Aerospace.

BROOKS: I don't believe anyone in our class has grandchildren. Cassie's still in kindergarten.

CHRIS: You were always retarded, Brooks.

BROOKS: When I went back for the tenth, all those married guys with their broods and their mortgages, they envied the shit out of me. I felt like a boy. They'd all gone to seed, fat, they looked fifty... And I was playing a lot of golf at the time, and I kept up my tan. They all had these wagons, half a block long, littered with old juice containers and parts of dolls and collapsible cribs, and I still had the red MG. I drove away from there, I tell you, I felt like a king.

EDDIE: Boy. That red MG. What ever happened to the old MG, Brooks?

BROOKS: Scrap.

EDDIE: You should have told me, Brooks. I would have bought it from you. For old time's sake.

EDDIE: Chris, do you remember Spring Trip Junior Year?

CHRIS: Like the back of my hand.

BROOKS: We went South. Willamsburg. Charleston.

EDDIE: Atlanta.

CHRIS: Talahassee. Fort Lauderdale.

EDDIE: You got in in Fort Lauderdale, didn't you, Brooksie?

BROOKS: No. But I got bare tit in Palm Beach. [*Pause.*] Or am I wrong, Chris? [*Pause.*] It seems like yesterday.

CHRIS: I loved those trips. The concerts. And the receptions outdoors. Those old alums pushing drinks on you, begging for another song. And you always knew, whatever horror show you put on, the bus was leaving the next morning and you could drink a bottle of beer or two in your seat and sleep.

EDDIE: I never did figure out how you slept through the Saint Mark's bridge game, Chris.

CHRIS: Leave the mess where it lay.

BROOKS: Little girl from Florida State or some goddamn place. Her hair loose and a corsage pinned to her shoulder. Looked like butter wouldn't melt in her mouth. First time I danced with her, though, I knew she was hot to trot. [*Pause.*] Madge wants to go back to school.

EDDIE: That'll teach you to rob the cradle.

BROOKS: To be a psychiatric social worker or some damn thing. I put my foot down. If we needed the money, I said, it would be a different story. But we don't and we've got two kids under seven and damn it they need their mother. Ask anybody.

EDDIE: Betsy's into martial arts. So I'm told.

BROOKS: Of course we could use the money. Who couldn't use a little extra money? But the kids come first.

CHRIS: You know what I miss most? The dancing. The waltzes. Why doesn't anybody waltz any more?

BROOKS: They do, Chris. It's coming back.

CHRIS: Not in time.

EDDIE: It's true, though. You know what Petey wants for his birthday? A dinner jacket. I swear, I can't believe it. At his age, we were lucky to get Ed Junior into clean jeans.

BROOKS: How's he doing, Eddie?

EDDIE: Ed? Great. Just great. It just takes these kids a while to find their feet these days. I personally think it's a healthy thing.

CHRIS: Why doesn't anyone wear tails any more?

BROOKS: Nobody did then. Except the Glee Club.

CHRIS: I did. All the time.

BROOKS: Rarely to class, Chris.

CHRIS: I rarely got to class, Brooks.

EDDIE: [*To* CHRIS.] I always remember you in tails. Nobody wore tails the way you did. With your blond hair slicked back and your patent leather pumps. And that crazy opera cape. You always looked like something out of a Fred Astaire movie.

[*Pause.* CHRIS *turns, goes to the bar and begins to pour himself a drink.*]

BROOKS: Uh uh, Chris. That's a no-no.

[CHRIS *holds up a bottle of tonic water.*]

CHRIS: Eau de quinine. Zero proof. I may be plucky, but I'm not crazy.

[*The doorbell rings.*]

EDDIE: O.K.

[EDDIE *goes to the door and opens it. Enter* RICHARD.]

RICHARD: Sorry I'm late. All hell was breaking loose at the hospital.

EDDIE: That's O.K. No sweat.

CHRIS: We're not going any place.

EDDIE: Let me get your coat. I'm Eddie. We talked on the phone.

RICHARD: I remember.

EDDIE: This is Brooks. Chris. This is Charlie Taylor's nephew.

RICHARD: Richard Crewes.

EDDIE: Ex-Whiff.

[EDDIE *takes his coat.* RICHARD *is wearing hospital whites and has a beeper attached to his belt.*]

EDDIE: [*Cont'd.*] I'll hang it up.

BROOKS: When were you in New Haven?

RICHARD: I got out in '70.

BROOKS: Med School?

RICHARD: College. I was '74 in Med School.

CHRIS: A child, Eddie. They sent us a child.

EDDIE: You're killing us with those numbers, Richard.

RICHARD: Freud said there's no such thing as a joke.

BROOKS: Are you going into psychiatry, Dick?

RICHARD: No. Neurosurgery. I've given it a lot of thought. The hours are pretty regular. The money's terrific. And I've got really good hand-eye coordination.

[*Pause.* CHRIS *nods, then walks off humming.*]

BROOKS: Where did you go to Med School, Dick? Yale?

RICHARD: No. Harvard.

EDDIE: [*Returning.*] That's a word we don't mention much around here, fella.

[RICHARD *looks at him, then crosses to the dip and potato chips and eats hungrily.*]

RICHARD: Excuse me. I'm on my dinner break.

EDDIE: I could make you a sandwich. I think there's some bread in the house. And stuff. It may be a little old.

BROOKS: I saw that bread, Dick. You don't want it.

RICHARD: This is swell.

BROOKS: What about a brew?

RICHARD: A what?

EDDIE: A beer.

RICHARD: I'd better not. I haven't had much sleep this week and I'm afraid it would knock me on my ass. Have you got a soft drink? Coke? Gingerale? Anything. Water would be fine. [*He continues eating.*]

EDDIE: I'll look.

[*He crosses to the kitchen.* RICHARD *eats.*]

BROOKS: Med School. That's some grind, isn't it?

RICHARD: Not so bad. Unless I've blocked it out.

BROOKS: I've heard the first two years are a bitch. Eighteen hours a day, seven days a week. Make you memorize all the muscles of the eye.

CHRIS: Trick you into drinking urine.

RICHARD: What?

CHRIS: My father was a doctor. He was full of Med School stories.

RICHARD: Maybe then. Not now. The Dark Ages are over.

BROOKS: Still, they must keep you pretty busy. Can't leave you much time for singing.

RICHARD: Actually, I spend most of my spare time backpacking. We're into backpacking.

BROOKS: Who? You and Charlie Taylor?

RICHARD: No. Corinne and I. The girl I live with.

BROOKS: Your fiancée?

RICHARD: No. The girl I live with.

[*Pause. To* CHRIS, *who is humming.*]

RICHARD: [*Cont'd.*] Excuse me for asking, but have you been that color long?

CHRIS: All my life.

RICHARD: I mean the, uh, pallor.

[CHRIS *crosses to a mirror, studies himself in it, then crosses back to* RICHARD.]

CHRIS: Inherited. All the men in my family have porcelain skin.

[*Enter* EDDIE *with a Coke and more beer.*]

RICHARD: Do me a favor, will you . . .

CHRIS: Chris.

RICHARD: Chris. Get your blood pressure checked.

[CHRIS *crosses to a chair and sits.*]

CHRIS: That's a cheery note. Makes a man want to burst into song.

EDDIE: [*Entering with more dip.*] Hey. Hey, Richard. The ground rules here are absolutely no shop. And, believe me, you better stick to them unless you want Brooks here to start boring the shit out of you with talk of high adventure in the bond business. [*Pause.*] Here's your Coke.

RICHARD: Thanks. [*Of the dip.*] This is terrific. What's in it?

EDDIE: I don't know. It's left over from the old regime.

RICHARD: It's very tasty. [*He drinks.*]

BROOKS: Eddie probably told you, Dick. We lost our bass last week after—what?—twenty years together...

EDDIE: More. Twenty-five. Six.

CHRIS: Six.

BROOKS: Keeled over in his office with a massive coronary.

CHRIS: Listen to this, Richard. It'll interest you.

BROOKS: His wife and another couple came to pick him up for a Cuban meal.

EDDIE: Bill was into Cuban food in the fifties. Way before it became an in thing. Old Bill.

CHRIS: Always a pace setter.

BROOKS: Found him stone dead on the carpet. Like a beached whale, Ann said. It was quite a shock for her. You can imagine, Dick.

CHRIS: Let's make some music while the rest of us are still around. [*He takes out his pitch pipe.*]

RICHARD: Chris, look, I'm sorry I opened my mouth. It's just that I'm at the hospital all day it's hard to change gears.

CHRIS: That's all right. I envy your earnestness. I really do.

BROOKS: Hey, Chris.

[*He crosses to him.*]

CHRIS: Let's sing, for Christ's sake.

EDDIE: What do you know, Richard?

RICHARD: Name it.

EDDIE: We don't do a lot of modern stuff—show tunes and all that. We do more traditional music.

BROOKS: More classically oriented.

EDDIE: Do you know "My Cutie's Due on the Two Two Two?"

RICHARD: For sure. I know all the oldies. My roommate had me down as some kind of freak.

EDDIE: A freak?

RICHARD: It's his word. He was into entomology. Spiders. He kept them in a shoe box in his dresser. So who was he to talk?

EDDIE: Why don't we start with something slow to sort of get tuned up. You game for "Slow Motion," Richard?

RICHARD: Sure. [*Vocalizing.*] When big brown bears go woof, Ah me, When big brown bears go woof.

CHRIS: We usually take it a half-step down. Out of respect to my failing prowess.

RICHARD: Fine with me.

ALL: Slow motion time,
Jes' idle a trifle
Happy, content with
Slow motion time.
Folks often say
"You're crazy, you're lazy,"
They don't know, they won't go,
Slow motion time.
Dawdle all the day,
Yawn the hours away,
I'se sleepy, so tired,
Time for me to lay right down and
Relax myself,
Don't look 'round,
Jes' lie down,
Indolent, somnolent,
Slow motion time.

BROOKS: Hey. That's not bad.

EDDIE: That's good. Nice legato, Richard.

RICHARD: Thanks. [*Looks at his watch.*] You want to try the other one?

EDDIE: Sure. Just let me lubricate the old pipes. [*He takes a long swallow of beer.*]

CHRIS: We do this one in the original key.

BROOKS: We've been doing this so long together we probably put in lot of stuff that isn't strictly in the music.

RICHARD: That's O.K. I'll follow.

[CHRIS *blows his pitchpipe again. They sing. The three older men do movements—eye movements, hand movements, business with their drinks, etc.* RICHARD *stands still and sings. He sings much better than they do.*]

ALL: My cutie's due on the two two two
She'll be coming through on the big choo choo
She's been away for months
But I haven't cheated once
Stayed home nights
I didn't dance
Wasn't taking any chance
Didn't flirt
Though it hurt

RICHARD: Just couldn't do my little cutie dirt

ALL: The days are long, the nights are black
But I just know that she'll be back
Cause I love her and she loves me
So say, hey hey hey
Don't say there ain't no Santa Claus
I know goddamn well there is because
My cutie's due on the two two two
Today.

EDDIE: Hey. Pretty good blend.

CHRIS: [*To* RICHARD.] Comfortable for you?

RICHARD: Sure.

BROOKS: You want to try some of the, uh, moves this next time through, Dick?

RICHARD: Fine with me.

CHRIS: I'll give you your note.

RICHARD: Don't need it.

EDDIE: Well, I need a note.

[CHRIS *gives the notes.*]

ALL: Bright college years wth pleasure rife

The shortest, gladdest years of life
How swiftly are ye gliding by
O why does time so swiftly fly?
The seasons come, the seasons go
The earth is green or white with snow
But time and change can naught avail

RICHARD: [*Solo.*] To break those friendships formed at Yale

ALL: In after years should troubles rise
To cloud the blue of summer skies
How bright will seem through mem'ry's haze
Those happy, golden bygone days
So drink her down with Mory's Ale
For God, for country and for Yale
My cutie's due on the two two two
Today.

[*During the phrase "Mory's Ale," RICHARD'S beeper starts beeping.*]

RICHARD: [*Over the end of the song.*] Excuse me, Eddie. Eddie, where's the phone?

EDDIE: In the bedroom. In through there.

RICHARD: Thanks. [*Exit RICHARD into the bedroom.*]

BROOKS: [*After a pause.*] What do you think?

CHRIS: He's good.

EDDIE: I think he's terrific.

BROOKS: Not to speak ill of the dead, but he's a hell of a lot better than Bill. Billy had the range, the low notes, but he always sounded as if he had to clear his throat.

EDDIE: That was the booze. Many's the night I've seen him put away half a bottle of Scotch before dinner.

CHRIS: Every night of his life, God bless him.

BROOKS: My only question is, does he have the feeling? The spirit? He seemed a little . . . reserved.

EDDIE: Brooks, for crying out loud, that was his first time through. He's young. He'll get it.

BROOKS: Chris?

CHRIS: Fine with me.

BROOKS: Then it's unanimous. I don't think we have to bother with the urn and the black balls and all that.

[*Pause. Re-enter* RICHARD.]

BROOKS: Tell him, Eddie.

EDDIE: Congratulations.

RICHARD: For what?

EDDIE: You're our new bass. Unanimous. No abstentions.

RICHARD: Thanks. I appreciate it. I really do.

BROOKS: It's not a decision we came to lightly, Dick.

RICHARD: I'm sure it wasn't. Eddie, where's my coat?

EDDIE: We sometimes sing at a little gin mill midtown. At lunchtime. They have entertainment Tuesdays and Fridays. Usually Dixieland but sometimes it's us. They get a lot of the advertising crowd. No pay, but free lunch and all the booze you can hoist.

BROOKS: You can call in sick those afternoons.

RICHARD: That sounds swell, Eddie. Look. Where's my coat? I've got a sick woman on my hands.

EDDIE: Well, why didn't you say so? [*He goes to the closet.*] We rehearse. Wednesday nights at different houses. The person whose house it is supplies the refreshments. Not that we'd expect you to take a turn yet, seeing as how you're not established.

BROOKS: Next Wednesday chez Brooks. What do you drink, Dick? Dubonnet? Campari? You name it, I've got it.

RICHARD: Listen. I'm not sure yet about Wednesday. I'll call you.

EDDIE: [*Holding the coat.*] Why aren't you sure?

RICHARD: I have to be on call nights. I never know till the last minute.

EDDIE: That's not what you said on the phone.

RICHARD: Things change.

EDDIE: Sometimes you have emergencies.

RICHARD: Right. Look, I've really got to go.

BROOKS: We sing at private parties too. Always lots of unattached chicks.

RICHARD: Give me my coat, Eddie.

CHRIS: You don't like us much, do you, Richard? You think we're ridiculous.

RICHARD: No. Not at all. It's been terrific. Only, to be frank, I didn't realize it was going to be a regular thing.

EDDIE: A regular thing? Goddamn it, that's the whole point.

RICHARD: I'm sorry, Eddie.

EDDIE: I'll bet you are.

RICHARD: Please, can I just have my coat?

EDDIE: No.

RICHARD: What?

EDDIE: Don't worry. The wounded and dying can get along without you for two minutes.

RICHARD: Brooks, would you please ask him...

EDDIE: You come in here, you come highly recommended by a man, by Charlie Taylor, a man who's been my friend since before you were born. You come into my house, my home, you won't drink with us, you wolf down all the cheese dip...

RICHARD: This is ridiculous.

EDDIE: I don't give a flying fuck about the cheese dip. There's more where that came from don't you worry. But it's indicative. I'm talking about manners, Doctor. Simple, goddamn manners.

BROOKS: Give the boy his coat, Eddie.

EDDIE: I will. In a minute. I don't want his coat. I wouldn't be caught dead on skid row in a shitty coat like this.

RICHARD: Give me my coat, Eddie. I don't want to hurt you.

EDDIE: Doctor, you have hurt me. To the quick. Do you know where that is?

RICHARD: Eddie...

EDDIE: You know Yale turned down my kid? Turned him down flat. Didn't even put him on the waiting list. And he is a wonderful kid. I practically went down on my knees to the Dean. I told him there have been four generations of Knoxes at Yale. Not captains of anything, not Phi Beta Kappas, not the stars. You probably wouldn't notice them while they were there, but they turned into useful goddamn people. Who coughed up for the Class Fund even when the Market was shot to hell, who denied themselves. Not selfish people. I tell you, I went up for the Harvard Game this year and I looked at the young people around me in the stands and it could have been...N.Y.U. So what I'm saying is, Doctor—and I hope I'm not talking out of turn—what I'm saying is, they really lost something at that place these past years. And manners is only part of it. Here's your stupid coat. [*He gives* RICHARD *the coat and walks off.*] Go cure your patient.

BROOKS: Dick, look, I'm sorry. The thing with his son broke his heart.

EDDIE: No it didn't. It broke his grandfather's heart. It made me furious.

BROOKS: Don't take it personally.

RICHARD: Believe me, gentlemen, I won't. [*Exit* RICHARD.]

EDDIE: [*After a pause.*] Didn't even thank me for the Coke. Look. I'm sorry. A real horror show, right? But I swear to God, fellas...

BROOKS: What, Eddie?

EDDIE: Shit, I don't know.

BROOKS: Want a brew?

EDDIE: No, thanks.

BROOKS: [*After a pause.*] I'm going to take off, Eddie. It's late.

EDDIE: Hey, Chris?

CHRIS: Present.

EDDIE: Chris, sing something, will you, for crying out loud?

CHRIS: Sure, Eddie. If you like. What?

EDDIE: I don't know. Anything. You're the only one of us who ever had a real voice anyway.

[*Pause.* CHRIS *crosses to the bar, pours himself a drink from the tonic bottle, turns, and sings to* EDDIE.]

CHRIS: Mavourneen, mavourneen
Sure one kiss would be no sin,
For I love you, ayalh,
Your poor slave is Barney O'Flynn.

[*Pause. Lights down slowly. Blackout.*]

THE END

Cassandra Medley

DEARBORN HEIGHTS

CASSANDRA MEDLEY

Cassandra Medley's plays include, *Ms. Mae*, one of several individual sketches which comprise the Off-Broadway musical, *A... My Name Is Alice*, which received the 1984 Outer Drama Critics Circle Award, and is still touring regional theatres and Europe. Other plays include, *Ma Rose, Waking Women, By the Still Waters*, and *Terrain*, all presented and produced throughout the U.S. For her screenplay, *Ma Rose*, Cassandra was awarded the Walt Disney Screenwriting Fellowship, in 1990. She is also the recipient of the 1986 New York Foundation for the Arts Grant, and a New York State Counil on the Arts Grant for 1987, was a 1989 finalist for the Susan Smith Blackburn Award in Playwriting, won the 1990 National Endowment for the Arts Grant in Playwriting, the 1995 New Professional Theatre Award and the 1995 Marily Simpson Award. She teaches playwriting at Sarah Lawrence College and Columbia University and has also served as guest artist at the University of Iowa Playwrights Workshop.

CHARACTERS

GRACE   A very light-skinned African-American woman in her late 20's, early 30's. She is thin and rather "slight." She carries a studied "air" of self-conscious "refinement" and speaks with a soft, lilting Tennessee accent. She is dressed in the "dress up" style of the early 1950s. A close-fitting hat is banded around the top of her head, perhaps with a bit of a small veil attached. She wears summer net gloves, stockings with the seams down the back, 50's style high heels, a "smart summer suit" of the mass-produced variety based on "high fashion." Her pocket book, which usually dangles from her wrist, is resting in her lap.

CLARE   Dark-skinned African-American woman, same age as GRACE. Rather hefty with a deliberate "commanding" bravado that disguises her vulnerability underneath.

SETTING: *A "homestyle" diner in Dearborn Heights.*

TIME: *A mid-Summer Day, 1951*

GRACE *is seated at restaurant table. The table is draped in checkered cloth, napkin dispenser, a tiny vase with a single plastic flower stem. It should give the feeling of a "homestyle" restaurant-diner. Several shopping bags and packages surround* GRACE *underneath the table. She takes out a large, folded newspaper article from her purse, admires it. The Andrews Sisters' "I'll Be Seeing You in Apple Bloosom Time" plays in background, coming from an unseen juke box.* GRACE *is clearly waiting for someone, as she sips the lemon coke in front of her. A basket of fresh bread has been already placed before her. There is a second table setting with a second lemon coke placed across from* GRACE. *She should appear to be glancing out of an imaginary window. A few more beats and then suddenly her face lights up and she waves to someone unseen. She quickly folds her newspaper, returns it to her purse and waits. Sound of a* DOOR CHIME *jingling. Enter* CLARE, *dark-skinned Black woman, same age as* GRACE *and dressed in the same style.* CLARE *faces the audience.* GRACE *waves as though through a window and gestures.* CLARE *turns, crosses to the table with her shopping bags in tow.*

CLARE: [*Fanning her perspiration.*] Whew! If it ain't hot as all-get out, out there.

[*Smiling* GRACE *helps* CLARE *with the packages which they tuck underneath their seats.*]

GRACE: Oh, you should feel "Knoxville" you think this is aggravating! I thought moving to Michigan was my release from "the fiery furnace," I see I was mistaken...truth is I done pulled off my shoes ha...I'm [*Whispering.*] "in my stocking feet."

CLARE: Ha. Well, I'm 'bout to pull mine off right behind you girl. Got a bunion that's "sounding off" like a bugle at the V-E Day parade!

GRACE: [*Gazing around.*] Ain't this a sweet place?

CLARE: [*Glancing around.*] Well...yeah...I guess...I mean, why is it...well...empty?

GRACE: Chile, I come here everytime I come to Dearborn shopping.

CLARE: Oh?

GRACE: Copied their way of doing "tuna salad"...

CLARE: Where's the waitress hiding out? [*Looking around for a beat, she then smiles and gives a brief friendly nod to an unseen waitress in the distance.*] Oh...good...

GRACE: [*Indicating the drinks on the table.*] See? Got us our lemon cokes.

CLARE: [*Still staring out, puzzled.*] Y'see that?

GRACE: I been here couple times, trust me. I promise she won't be as slow as that salesgal in the "Lingerie Department."

CLARE: [*Distracted.*] Ummm? Don't mind me, girl, I just...well when a place is empty makes me "jittery"...[*She "cackles" with a wave of her hand.*]...Starts me to wonder "what am I gonna be spending my money on? Funny food or something...?"

[*Sound of a* DOOR CHIME *jingling.*]

GRACE: Ha...your turn to be the "stranger" and have me show "you" a new place!...See? Here come a couple of people...

CLARE: Oh! Wonderful! [*Settling into her seat, relaxing, buttering her bread.*] I am ready to "chow"—my stomach is about to "mutiny."

GRACE: [*Pause.*] Well what happened? What did I miss?

CLARE: Humph! The "so and so" of ah Floor Manager finally decided to put in a appearance...

GRACE: [*Glancing at her watch.*] Girl, I was wondering if I should have the waitress hold the table. I started to go back 'cross the street to check on you...wondered how long they'd keep you waiting.

[CLARE *stops and reaches down into her packages. She pulls out a box and reveals a pair of long white evening gloves. She salutes* GRACE *"army" style.*]

CLARE: "Mission accomplished" under enemy fire.

GRACE: [*Impressed.*] Well!

CLARE: I tole you if I waited there long enough and held out for that store manager...

GRACE: [*Overlapping.*] And they finally let you exchange them for the right fit?

CLARE: That's right! Boils me how they try and treat "us" when we shop in these suburbs...

GRACE: Well, I'm impressed...

CLARE: They up there trying to tell me they "can't exchange my gloves cause they was purchased in the De-troit Montgomery Wards and not this here Dearborn Heights branch of Mongtomery..."

GRACE: [*Overlapping.*]...Wards

CLARE: Yeah, you heard they "crap!" That's all it was! "Crap."

GRACE: [*Glancing at the menu.*]...You gonna have fries or...you still on your diet...?

CLARE: [*Putting on one of the formal gloves as she speaks.*] I just explained to them with a smile on my face [*She illustrates "smile."*]

that fine, "I will make sure to write *The Chronicale*, Michigan's largest Negro newspaper, and to tell all my church members to make sure not to shop at Montgomery Wards period."

GRACE: That did it, huh?

CLARE: And I tole him, I say, "You know Wards got no business putting better quality merchandise in the Dearborn stores then they got in the Detroit stores ANWAY"...like we "enjoy" driving out all this way into the suburbs just to get us decent...

GRACE: Well it's so "pretty" out this way...but no—you right... you right...

CLARE: [*Pauses, shrugs.*] I guess they just figured, "Let's just get this colored bitch out the way, what the hell."

GRACE: Nunno! No! What you did was...y'know...I admire...I mean...anything large or small that we do for the "Race"...

CLARE: [*Carefully packing the gloves back in their box, then taking up her menu.*] Dearborn is a very long way to come to shop if you don't drive...

GRACE: Is it? [*Pause.*]...Driving out here with you was nice, but I like the bus...I don't mind...[*Stiffly smiling.*]

[*The* DOOR CHIME *sounds again as other unseen customers enter.*]

CLARE: [*Smiling.*] Ha. [*Pause.*] That is one "sharp" hat you got... been meaning to tell you all morning...

GRACE: [*Touching her hat, smiling.*] Oh, I collect hats, I love hats... thank you...you so sweet...didn't know if I should wear it just for shopping.

CLARE: It's gorgeous on you girl! If you "got it" why not "flaunt it."

GRACE: People...well...don't want folks to think one is you know...[*She makes a silent gesture to indicate "stuck on oneself."*] ...people can think things you know...

CLARE: [*Placing her hand on top of* GRACE'S *hand.*] Girl...when that Moving Van pulled up and you and your husband got out... and next thing I know there you are out there putting in rose bushes along ya driveway, and I thought to myself, "thank you, Jesus"...cause, see, we on our street are "vigilant"...the last thing we want is a bunch of "sorry," shiftless Colored Folk "ruining" what we all trying to build!

GRACE: Didn't mean for two months to go by 'fore I came over.

CLARE: You're a little on the "shy side" ain't ya?

GRACE: [*Smiles.*] My husband teases me...I thought you maybe thought...took it for granted I was...you know...[*She makes a gesture to indicate "stuck up."*]

CLARE: [*Smiling, waving off suggestion.*] Childe, pal-lease! Okay, now the question is do I have the "BLT" dripping in mayo or...

GRACE: Oh, and "by the by"...they delivering me and O.Z.'s new television set tomorrow...

CLARE: Well, ah right!

GRACE: [*Pauses, rather uncertain.*] Well, yeah...I think I'm gonna "miss" the radio...

CLARE: Now you can keep up with that crazy "Lucy" every week...

GRACE: Something, well, I dunno, something "cultivated" 'bout the radio.

CLARE: Chile, last night, "Lucy" dyed her hair jet black, would you believe, and "Desi" got hisself on this "quiz show" he had no business fooling with...oh, they had me "in stiches" so I nearly choked to death!..."Cultivated"...[*Pause.*] You got such a... "sweet" way with words. I been admiring all morning how you..

GRACE: Some Negroes get excellent educations down South contrary to what you might hear 'bout us!

CLARE: 'Course you gotta be "word-fancy" if you gonna qualify as "telephone operator." [*Graciously.*] Oh, we must order something extra special, you're my first new girlfriend to celebrate!

[GRACE *offers a toast with her coke.*]

CLARE: [*Cont'd.*] I'm living right next door to "one of the first five Negro women to be hired by the phone company." I tole my Momma 'bout it.

GRACE: Ah, ain't you sweet! Ain't you the sweetest thing!

CLARE: Well, the whole entire street is proud! My goodness! [*Pause.*]

You make sure you preserve that pic-ture they had of you in the "Chronicale" for your children. [*Pause, staring at her.*] 'Bout time some Negro women got hired to do something more worthwhile than that ole "mop and pail" stuff I be doing up at the Hospital!

[*They toast with their lemon cokes. Pause.*]

CLARE: [*Cont'd.*] I tell you, here I am living right next door to a Negro Pioneer!

GRACE: Truth be told, when I went for the interview my hands were shaking so ... I could barely hear my voice.

CLARE: Who cares? For the very first time in De-troit, whenever we call "directory assistance" it could be one of five new Negro operators ... could be you ... don't worry ... if I recognize your voice I won't "chat". ... I know how to act as opposed to "some" of our people ...

GRACE: [*Graciously.*] Well, now, you got something to be proud of yourself now ... standing up for yourself like that! ... Whew! That's what I luv 'bout being up North! Back down in Knoxville you wouldn't dare ... they don't even allow us to try the clothes on, just have to take your chances ... and you don't dare return it if it don't fit ...

CLARE: Well, I am proud to say I've never been "South" of Dayton, Ohio, where I'm from.

GRACE: [*Glancing over the menu.*] This being our first shopping trip together and a day of celebration ... I say we "sin" and have hot fudge sundays ...

[*The DOOR CHIME sounds again as other unseen customers enter.*]

CLARE: Let's see the pic-ture.

GRACE: Well, I dunno ... I mean ...

CLARE: Naw-naw ... don't you carry it 'round with ya? I would, you couldn't stop me from showing it 'round if it was "me". ...

GRACE: We don't want folks accusing me of the "sin of pride," now do we?

CLARE: So how's your hubby liking driving for the Bus Company? 'Course, my Clyde's got "lifetime" job security at Chryslers ...

[GRACE *takes out a folded newsprint photo from her purse and hands it over to* CLARE.]

CLARE: [*Cont'd. Reading from the paper.*] "July 23, 1952"... Course, I have my own copy back at the house...

GRACE: Ain't you the sweetest thing! [*Pause.*]

CLARE: Some Colored folks might think I was causing too much of a "rucus" over a pair of gloves...

GRACE: Girl, you don't know me! [*Laughing.*]... Wait till you get to know me better... I admire "spunk," "grit" as we call it back down home.

CLARE: Well, like you say... our very first "girls day out"... didn't wanna embarrass you.

GRACE: The first of many!

[*They toast.*]

CLARE: Folks keep staring at us, Grace... don't look...

[GRACE *on reflex reaches her hand to her hat to make sure it's on right. DOOR CHIME sounds.* CLARE *slowly gazes around. The DOOR CHIME jingles as more unseen patrons enter. There is the soft sound of murmuring.*]

CLARE: [*Cont'd.*] Act like nothing's wrong.

GRACE: What is wrong?

CLARE: Oh, gawd...

GRACE: What?

CLARE: Oh, mercy.

GRACE: What is it?

CLARE: Oh, Jesus, my Jesus... don't stare! Sorry, but... don't let 'em know we know.

GRACE: What? What do we know?

CLARE: Girl, you made a mistake in coming to this place...

GRACE: You don't mean

CLARE: That's right, that's the ticket alright...

GRACE: But...

CLARE: Everybody else is being served over there, over there... over there...

GRACE: But they served me: they always serve...

[*Embarassed pause between the two women.*]

CLARE: Well! [*Pause.*] I guess they realize now that they "took a few things for granted" didn't they?

GRACE: Oh, God.

CLARE: You had them "fooled."

GRACE: Gawd!

CLARE: Now they realize you—

GRACE: Don't "say" it—

CLARE: Ain't the shade they "assumed" you was.

GRACE: Jesus in Heaven.

CLARE: We better call on somebody.

GRACE: [*Mortified.*] Clare, I'm so... I'm so...

CLARE: Nunno, don't get up. Don't let 'em think "we know."

GRACE: Least down South they got... we got "signs" up.

CLARE: Well, I never been down South, couldn't drag me down South.

GRACE: I'm still not used to dealing with up "here"... the signals to go by... that waitress has always been so nice to me... how could I be so stupid...

CLARE: KEEP YOUR SEAT... keep your face in the menu for the time being... [*Pause.*] ... We came here to have "lunch" and by-golly have lunch is what we gonna "have." They'll have to serve us or throw us out! [*Pause.*] Now then...

[CLARE *reaches into her bag and pulls out a ribboned broach the size of a small badge. She hands it to* GRACE.]

CLARE: [*Cont'd.*] ..."The Southwest Detroit Ladies Cavaliers" wants to welcome you as a new member!

[GRACE *distractedly waves off broach.*]

GRACE: Shouldn't we just get up and go...

CLARE: [*Reaching down.*] Don't look around...pretend nothing's wrong. [*Smiling self-consciously.*]...now, uh, the "grapevine" tells me you being, uh...shall we say "approached" by the "Metropolitan Ladies of Triumph"...

GRACE: Well...they have, you know...uh...

CLARE: Oh, I know, they "after ya" right? They always scrounging 'round for "new blood" like "gnats at a picnic"...not that I'm bragging but they ain't the Ladies Club for a Colored Woman of "quality"...believe me...

GRACE: Look, why cause a whole lotta fuss? Let's just...

CLARE: Keep smiling so they don't know we're upset...hate it when Colored People don't know how to keep their dignity in public?...

GRACE: I am so so embarassed! [*Pause.*] How do you tell up North where "we" can go and can't go?

CLARE: Grace, you gotta learn the difference 'tween De-troit and the suburbs—Detroit and Dearborn, Dearborn and Detroit...me being President of Cavaliers means I can, you know, "guide" you more easily than they can in "Ladies of "Triumph"...[*Pause.*] Relax...lean back, let 'em know we ain't to be "budged" and we ain't to be "bothered!" Now, then. [*Pause.*] Every year we "Cavaliers" happen to raise more than "Ladies of Triumph" do for the NAACP...why, "they" was so "low-class" they held they "Annual Fashion Show" at the "Y." "We" at least rent the Elks Lodge over on Livernois and 9 Mile...

GRACE: "Up North" was supposed to be so 'easy'...come to find out it's even more complicated...

CLARE: You just gotta fine-tune your sense of place! Look for other Negroes, and if you don't sense 'em there, then they don't want us there. Feel out the air around you!...We sponsor this "Gospel Jubillee" in the Spring that'll send you to Heaven and back...

GRACE: Down South it is clearly marked...please, please pardon me...

CLARE: It is very unusual for any "newcomer" to get a "unanimous" vote from our membership.

GRACE: I shoulda sensed something...no wonder everybody's sitting so spread out away from this table...Lord, the "cook" is peering out at us from the kitchen...!

CLARE: Let him...see when "we" shop in these here suburbs we gotta be armour plated inside girl...Don't let "them" push us around...! That's the spirit of a Lady in "Cavaliers"! [*Pause.*] Plus, as an added bonus...I'll teach you how to drive...guarantee you'll pass "the road test"...and don't you dare ask me to accept no fee! [*She guffaws softly.*]

GRACE: My man's the, you know, the basic "Ole-fashioned" Southern type...he prefers to do the driving in our—

CLARE: Chile, you up North now! We the "New Negro" women up here!...[*Leaning in on her and softly poking her.*] I can tell ya want to...tell the truth...ain't you tempted by just a itty-bitty bit of independence?

GRACE: Thing of it is, they know me here!...The waitress is "Mattie" over there...told me all 'bout her "bunions"...even promised me the recipe for "chicken-a-la-king"...

CLARE: "Mattie," huh? Ooough! If I just had it "in" me to "lay her out" to her face!

GRACE: Clare, please...

CLARE: I'm not blaming you—don't think that, you made a honest mistake...but, see now this is the very reason why you need to join us "Cavaliers."

GRACE: [*Graciously smiling.*]...To tell the truth, very soon I'm gonna be in need of the "restroom facilities"...oh otherwise I'd be all for sitting this out...[*Pause.*] 'Sides, [*Smiling.*] I seriously doubt if I'm gonna be able to, you know, "receive" the proper "impression" of Calaviers—I don't think your Club Members want me to be famished in the process...

CLARE: ...[*Pause.*] Ha. [*Pause.*] Sweetness [*Pause.*] Let us leave this minute! Please—please pardon me!

GRACE: Nunno, I'm the one got us into this—

CLARE: Nunno..."last" thing I want is for you to be put through...

you know ... stress and strain and, and "devil-made" connip-
tions 'cause of "yours truly" ... please ...

GRACE: Nunno ... it's "my" fault ... but, we'll just take our stom-
achs and our business to where we can get respect AND so we
can concentrate ... ha ...

CLARE: Fine ... All we need to do is just "maneuver" out of this here
with some lil bit of "dignity" ...

GRACE: Just follow me to the door ...

CLARE: Don't panic ... worst thing is to panic ... compose your face
'fore you get up ...

GRACE: Everybody's eyeing us ... oh, Gawd ... The longer we sit
here it's just more awful!

CLARE: I will not give them the "satisfaction" of seeing me panic ...
think they gonna "run me out" oh, naw! Get up when I'm good
and ready, "my time, not they time" ... Grace, control yourself!

GRACE: All their eyes trained on us!

CLARE: My dear, just gimme one second ... Don't come unstuck ...
you are not "down South," now. Just keep a steady hand till I
get my shoes on ...

GRACE: Fine—fine. Long as we don't get into no more monkey
business foolishness, let's go.

CLARE: Wha kinda "business," excuse me?

GRACE: Clare ... please ...

CLARE: Please "explain" that last remark ... calmly compose your
face, and then we will rise and get out of here.

GRACE: [*Pause.*] There is no need for you to "order" me around in
such fashion.

CLARE: [*Taking a long gulp from her glass.*] Sons-of-bitches! [*To*
GRACE.] Excuse me, pardon me.

GRACE: Nunno, under the circumstances I'd say the same 'cept I
got too much of the "church woman" in me.

[*They pat each other's hands in mutual comfort.*]

CLARE: I'll sit here as long as I can stand it—ain't gonna run me off like no "whipped mongrel!"

GRACE: Thing of it is, they don't... they don't snarl at us, or... or yell at us, or attack in the same way they do down home.

CLARE: No, I will not just "fold my tent" and like a lamb, "bleet" all the way home... Oh, it gauls me... but, they ain't gonna break me...!

GRACE: Pardon me, but there is no need to make the situation any worse.

CLARE: I'm the "dark" one that's gotta get past their stares, walk through to that door over there!

GRACE: Now, hold up Clare Henderson... just 'cause I'm light don't mean I'm not feeling the same as your feeling!

CLARE: [*Overlapping.*] Take it easy... Nobody's saying nothing 'bout your...

GRACE: Well, what are you saying?

CLARE: Well, who you calling a "monkey?"

GRACE: Now, wait a minute here! We are not gonna lower ourselves to such a "level," now are we?

CLARE: Look, if the "boot" fits then march in it!

GRACE: [*Pauses, then.*] Well! Trouble is "your kind" gets so...

CLARE: So?

GRACE: "Wound-up."

CLARE: [*Folding her arms.*] Here we go! I knew you'd get to it sooner or later... the "darker" we come, the more we embarrass you, huh?

GRACE: Look, I'm the one they treated so nice "before."

CLARE: Before me.

GRACE: Before!

CLARE: You wouldn't be treated like a leper "now" if I wasn't sitting up here, would ya?

GRACE: You think it's easy? D'you think it's easy being taken for granted as "one thing" then facing the "flip" look when...

CLARE: Then you knew they was "taking it for granted," yet you lead me in here!

GRACE: [*Putting on her gloves, grabbing her packages to leave.*] I made an honest mistake. I'm "new" in this here city, if you have the "decency" to recall.

CLARE: I got the "decency to recall" that soon as you and your high yella Clark Gable "wannabe" husband moved on the block you've had your noses tipped in clouds, so high and mighty! [*Pause.*] Oh, yeah, anything to lord yaselfs over the whole entire street! The Block votes to get all new "look alike" Lamp Lighter Front Porch Lamps in front of each and every house, like in the white suburbs. But, naw—naw! You and your husband gotta do something "fancier," something more "high toned"—just a tad one step above the rest.

GRACE: Humph!... Why don't you get yourself a "telescope" out of one of them Sears catalogues so you can keep your "busy-body" nose better in everybody's business? A neighbor can't "sneeze" and you report it to everyone!

CLARE: [*Pauses... Studies* GRACE *with contempt.*] And to think you had me "groveling"... at your feet to... [*She snatches up the club brooch.*] ... oh, all them "begged" me to take you out, show you shopping... lunch you as "our treat"... but I tole 'em, I said, "I wonder if she's not too siddity, too "high-toned" and stuck up for us.

GRACE: You are so damn "pushy" who would want to "join?" [*Reaches for her bags under the table.*]

CLARE: Damn, you red-bone, "high yella," "lemon meringues" always the first to be hired to the best jobs... always flaunting ya color, and every other Negro fawning over ya'!

GRACE: That's right! "Vanilla" still beats out "chocolate" any day!

CLARE: Every night probably get down on ya damn knees and pray, "thank you, Jesus, for making me light, bright and almost white."

[*A pause, then.*]

GRACE: Is that what you would do in my place?

CLARE: [*Stunned a little, but struggles to hide it.*] I tole the Cavaliers you had no intentions of joining us anyway... [*She starts putting on her gloves.*]... Or do you think it entirely "escapes" me that the Ladies of Triumph all happen to be just about as "pale" as they can find 'em?

GRACE: [*Remains stock still.*] Nobody's telling me I ain't a dedicated Negro woman, same as you!

CLARE: Ha..."dedicated"!? [*Mocking GRACE.*] "Lez go, lez go, 'fore we cause mo' trouble"... You can't wait to go "shuffling" out of here with your tail between you legs... [*Pause.*] So your lil "diner" friends have "let you down"... well, "ta-ta"... [CLARE *gestures dismissively to* GRACE.]

GRACE: Hell with you, I'll sit as long as I want to!

CLARE: Fact is, the rest of "us"... don't want y'all "high tone types"... don't need ya...

GRACE: Oh, you want us, you crave us... don't blame us if you fawn all over us...

CLARE: Y'all don't have no real idea what real "color" feels like.

GRACE: And you do?... You, and the way you just had to "throw your weight around" in that store 'bout those "gloves"... not the principle of the thing I minded, but you had to be so loud, so "pronounced" about it...

CLARE: I? I was "standing up for something!" [*Gesturing with her gloved hand.*] But, of course, you got treated way, way more "courteous" by the salesgal... Guess you thought I didn't notice?

GRACE: I noticed that the other Colored shoppers were "cringing," but, of course, you thought you were "displaying" your courage in front of each and every damn body...

CLARE: [*Coolly lights a cigarette and studies* GRACE.] What's it like being "accepted" everywhere you go?

GRACE: And what the hell is that supposed to mean?

CLARE: Taken for "granted" as just a... you know... "normal," everyday, "pretty woman"... what's it feel like?

GRACE: Don't you dare start "toying with me"...

CLARE: Since I'm so "bossy," and "nosey," I'm gonna be sure and tell the "whole block"...

[CLARE *pauses, smiling with a sardonic expression on her face.* GRACE *rises to leave.*]

GRACE: [*Mocking expression*] You are such a "small-minded" woman.

CLARE: Why, sure not as sharp as you, girl. After all, as you say yourself, "they know you here," right? What's it been like? Lemme guess...here you ain't been in De-troit two months and ya already staked out a "nice" friendly, "homestyle diner" in Dearborn Heights where you "treat" yourself to cool, restful summer lunches...[*Pause.*] Tell me, what's it been like, Grace, so I can tell the whole street!

GRACE: No, hold up...! It...has never been my intention that I was...

CLARE: What's that? Sorry, I'm too "simple-minded..."

[GRACE'S *face contorts in sudden shock and pain. She drops her head in silence. A long beat. Suddenly a tight smile crosses* GRACE'S *face.*]

GRACE: Don't try and pull that outlandish crap on me.

CLARE: So she does her passing on a "shopping spree" to the suburbs, now don't that beat all!

GRACE: You the one who would want to wouldn't ya?...not me.

CLARE: How many afternoons do ya treat yaself to "make believing" you a white "heifer?"

GRACE: Wouldn't you just like to know...wouldn't you just like to be able to "dress yaself" in my dreams?!

CLARE: Thank God I was born with some real "paint" on my bones, and not no poor "in-between!" Lease way's when folks "see" me they know what side of the fence I'm looking back from!

GRACE: "Fence"!? Oh, and don't you just wish you could "open the gate"! Don't try and tell me you don't just wish you could scrub even just a "layer" of that...

CLARE: [*She is visibly trembling, but softly taunting* GRACE.] And we all know how ya got that "shade" of grey.

GRACE: ...a layer of that "dirt color" down the drain. [*She is trem-*

bling.] ... don't care how much "face cream" and lipstick you put on ...

CLARE: [*Trembling and smiling a fierce vicious smile.*] Generations of "poon-tag" raped and put out on the market...

GRACE: ... and "rouge" and ... and eye-shadow, and "Nu-nile" gloss on that nappy, hot-combed head, you still ain't gonna be close to being...

CLARE: [*Hurt, but taunting.*] The real "true" woman you get to be everytime you "escape"... right? right? And you thank God you can "escape"... don't cha! Don't cha!

GRACE: [*Nodding*] Absolutely... Abso... [*Realizing what she's saying, she cringes, drops her head.*]

[*Suddenly there is a ground swell of sound. The unseen* WHITE PATRONS *begin banging tableware against glassware to protest* GRACE *and* CLARE'S *presence. They both look up startled.*]

CLARE: [*Softly, grabbing* GRACE'S *hand.*] Don't turn around Grace... don't let them see your fear...

GRACE: But what if they... if they grab us... if they punch us...

CLARE: They too "gen-teel" for that... we're just "women" and it's just two of us... they won't go too far. [CLARE *lifts her glass and shouts out loud, facing the audience.*] Well, I got a lemon Coke out of it, nothing you can do about that can ya'!! Smash the glass, but you can't take the Coke back!!

UNSEEN VOICE: Get on back to De-troit where you niggers belong!

[GRACE *takes a long sweeping look at the audience, she stares at* CLARE *as they gather their packages.*]

GRACE: Oh, it "gauls me"... oh, it "gauls me."

CLARE: [*Softly smiling.*] Welcome to the "Motor Capital of the World."

[*They rise together. They stare out at the audience as they clutch each other's arms and hold their heads high. They take slow steps towards the audience. Soft "CACKYLING" from an unseen "crowd" can be heard in background. They take slow dignified steps towards the audience. They "cross" a lighted boundary, the DOOR CHIME "sounds,"*]

TRAFFIC NOISE, they are standing face front to the audience with the impression that they are now outside the diner. They still clutch each other for a few moments, then pull away.]

CLARE: [*Panting.*] Feels like I'm a icicle all over.

GRACE: My heart's racing... racing

CLARE: Lemme just stop shaking... ha...

GRACE: My heart's pounding...

CLARE: [*Suddenly checks her packages.*] Did we get everything, Grace? ... [*Quickly counting her packages. Pause. Frantically.*] Whew!... We made it... ha... one day we'll tell our kids how we stood up to the crackers one summer day in Dearborn Heights!

[*It is obvious they are too embarrassed to look each other in the face.*]

GRACE: [*Pause, then.*] To think all that ugly could come out of my mouth...

CLARE: All that trash I was talking... please... don't see how you could ever "pardon" me...

[GRACE *tries to answer, cannot.*]

CLARE: [*Cont'd., soft.*] Did I have all the Colored cringing back at Montgomery Wards?

GRACE: [*Turning to her.*] Nunno... you stood up for...

CLARE: [*Overlapping.*] ... No, you were right... I embarrassed everybody...

GRACE: Colored Rights!

CLARE: I was so—so loud and bodacious... tell me true now...

GRACE: What could I say to you that you could possibly believe after today? [*Staring out in a daze.*] They... they... got to see the... "base" side of us, that's what gets to me.

CLARE: [*Pause.*] You left me standing there at the counter, I must have been behaving pretty awful.

GRACE: [*Pause.*] Clare [*Pause.*] understand something... I may have "crossed" the Mason-Dixon line, but it's still in me... Even when I take the long ride out here on the bus, just to go past all the lovely homes and gardens? Still can't even bring myself to take a seat, sit "up front" even though I know we're "allowed" to up North, here... and I can't even tell my husband that.

[*They both smile to each other a moment.*]

CLARE: Know what we need? [*Pause.*] We need ta "shop" all this outta our system... calm our nerves.. haha... Okay Hudson's, here we come... gonna get me some new patten-leather heels right now! Where'd I park m'car? I'm so frazzled...

[CLARE *begins to move off,* GRACE *stops her with her voice.*]

GRACE: First time I went there I really didn't "think" of it as "passing"... [*Pause.*] But then again, didn't I? And then the next time... and then the next...

CLARE: Don't start "unraveling" nothing!... Leave where it lays, forget it took place, come on...

GRACE: But... truth be told... when I really deep down think about it...

CLARE: [*Smiling.*] Oh, to hell with the "truth"... thinking too much frays the nerves, don't you know that...

GRACE: Clare...! [*Pause.*] Everytime we meet up, "today" is gonna be "behind" our eyes, our... smiles... our "hellos."

[GRACE *grabs* CLARE'S *hand for a moment as they still look away. Embarrassed,* CLARE *pats* GRACE'S *hand, gently pulls off and "brightens."*]

CLARE: Now, we gonna get the car, get back cross the line to Detroit and get us some food in us 'fore we faint from this heat...

GRACE: Will I tell O.Z. about today, I wonder? Will you tell Clyde?

CLARE: I always say it's a wise woman who charts a clear course 'tween women's business and men's.

GRACE: Now, if I join up with Cavaliers you'll probably think—

CLARE: No, I will not.

GRACE: I'm feeling obliged in some way...

CLARE: No, you mistake... I DON'T INTEND TO "THINK" ABOUT IT EVER... [*Pause.*] I guess I "push against" folks... so I don't break... [*Pause.*] Never let nothing BREAK ME... I

JUST—I JUST [*Pause. Studies* GRACE, *then.*]...I say we "toss" this whole day in the pile marked "never happened" and stop feeding on it, period...

GRACE: It's not just gonna dissolve away.

CLARE: Don't fool yaself...pieces fall away bit by bit, 'till finally it's just a haze of a recollection way, way back...then, presto, it never happened.

GRACE: [*Pause.*] Wonder if one day we might end up "real buddies?"...

CLARE: [*Pause. Smiling.*] Could be dangerous to your home life. [*Pause, smiles.*]...For one thing, you just might end up learning how to drive.

GRACE: [*Giggling.*] Ha. [*Then, she suddenly turns somber.*]..."Toss it back and forget it ever happened...?"

[*Pause. They stare off in different directions.* GRACE *removes her sunglasses from her purse, puts them on.* CLARE *takes out her compact, checks her face.*]

CLARE: [*Her face is a smiling "mask."*] I already have...

GRACE: [*Pause, then.*] "Dearborn Heights."

Fade out.

END OF PLAY

Lavonne Mueller

AMERICAN DREAMERS

LAVONNE MUELLER

Lavonne Mueller is currently New Plays Editor of Applause Books. Her play, *Letters to a Daughter From Prison*, about Nehru and his daughter, Indira, was produced at the First International Festival of the Arts in New York City and went on to tour in India. Her play, *Violent Peace*, was produced in London in 1992 and was the "Critics Choice" in *Time Out Magazine*. Her play, *Little Victories*, was produced in Tokyo by Theatre Classic Productions and directed by Riho Mitachi. Her play, *The Only Woman General*, was produced in New York City and went on to the Edinburgh Festival, where it was "Pick of the Fringe" by the Scotland critics. She was awarded the Roger Stevens Playwriting Award, which she received at the Kennedy Center in Washington, DC, in 1992. She is a Woodrow Wilson Scholar, a Lila Wallace Reader's Digest Writing Fellow, and has received a Guggenheim Grant, a Rockefeller Grant, three National Endowment for the Arts Grants, a Fulbright to Argentina, an Asian Culture Council Grant to Calcutta, India, and a U.S. Friendship Commission Grant to Japan. Her plays have been published by Dramatist Play Service, Samuel French, Applause Books, Performing Arts Journal, Theatre Communication Group, Heinemann Books, and Baker's Plays. Her textbook, *Creative Writing*, published by Doubleday and The National Textbook Company, is used by students around the world. She has been an Arts America speaker for the USIS (United States Information Service) in India, Finland, Romania, Japan, Yugoslovia, and Norway. She was recently a Fulbright Fellow to Jordan and received a National Endowment for the Humanities grant to do research in Paris during the summer of 1995.

CHARACTERS

MARILYN MONROE   age 36
CARL SANDBURG   vigorous 70-plus

TIME: *August 1, 1962, 11:30 pm*
PLACE: *A hotel suite in Washington, D.C.*

AT RISE: We see MARILYN *sitting before a Russian samovar. Next to the samovar are colorful folk-painted cups with the letter "C" on them. There are five phones scattered throughout the room. A large saucer-like bulging disk is on the wall over the head of the bed. From the window we can see the Capitol Building.* MARILYN *is wearing a black dress with pearls. Her blond hair is up in a twist. We see* MARILYN *look at her watch impatiently. Then she goes to the phone and calls downstairs to the hotel desk.*

MARILYN: This is 508. I'm expecting a Mr. Sandburg. [*A beat.*] Are you sure? [*A beat.*] You can't miss him. He's muscular with bushy white hair. [*As she is waiting for the desk to look for Sandburg, she walks to the window and admires the view of the Capitol Building. Then, into the phone.*] You have two fat men with bushy white hair? No, I don't see why I should talk to them. They're not Sandburg, I guarantee you. But thanks, anyway.

[*She hangs up. She goes to the window and stares out again. Then she looks at her watch. She goes to the table and picks up her pen and doodles on a piece of paper. Then she goes to the door and looks both ways down the hall. She goes to the phone.*]

[*Into the phone.*] This is room 508 again. I'm still waiting for Mr. Sandburg. He should have been here an hour ago. He's never late. I'm the one who should be late. [*A beat.*] Yes . . . yes . . . yes . . . that's right. Bushy white hair. He's probably carrying Schopenhauer. [*A beat.*] Over by the main door? Go grab him. I'll wait.

[*She swings her foot impatiently, then examines the very high spike heels she is wearing. She squints at the heels, then kicks them off and walks to the sofa where there is a shoe box on the sofa. She takes out a pair of very conservative pumps with one-inch heels. She puts them on.*]

[*Rattles into the phone without taking a breath.*] Yes. I'm still here. Wonderful. Let me talk to him. [*A beat.*] Carl? Of all times for you to be late. I have so much to tell you. I figured your poetry reading ran over time at the White House? Right? Just hurry on up... [*She opens the door just a crack as she holds the phone. Into the phone.*] What? [*A beat.*] Who are you? [*A beat.*] Otis Sprague? [*A beat.*] You have a lot of muscles and thick white hair? Please put the Desk back on the phone. [*A beat.*] Desk? I don't want a Sprague. [*A beat.*] Yes... yes... I know I asked for muscular.

[*We see* CARL *come in the partially opened door. He puts his guitar inside by the door. He stands by the door only partially seen. His hair is combed back very smoothly and he is wearing a tux. He stands listening to* MARILYN.]

MARILYN: [*Cont'd.*] The man I want is bushy. With tufts of cactus spiking out over his forehead. Worse than Robert Frost. Worse than Albert Sweitzer, even. You'd never know he writes poetry. He looks like a drifter.

CARL: I am a drifter.

MARILYN: [*Looks at* CARL *and smiles. Into phone.*] Never mind. I've found him. [*She hangs up.*]

CARL: Poor Mr. Sprague. Did he know for one shining moment he was talking to Marilyn Monroe?

MARILYN: You'll be glad to know I'm not the same Marilyn.

CARL: What's wrong with America is not Marilyn Monroe.

MARILYN: Not Carl Sandburg, either. But America only needs one of us. [*A beat.*] Did you see Him?

CARL: I saw Her. [*A beat.*] Like the tux?

MARILYN: Frankly, no.

CARL: She did. [*A beat.*] Poets can be sex objects, too. Except for her, I was wasted tonight at the White House on a lot of cranky old senators.

MARILYN: You look like a wai...

[CARL *cuts her off and they both say "waiter" together.*]

CARL: Have you fallen into platitudes?

MARILYN: I've always liked waiters.

CARL: When's the last time you married one?

MARILYN: Carl, please sit down. I want to hear all about your poetry reading. And tonight...we don't have loads of time like we usually do.

CARL: [*Clears his throat and reads formally from a paper he takes out of his jacket.*]
When Lincoln makes love
there's only bread.
Ink and blood run down his chin
the juice of a failure.
His dead
take away the butter.

MARILYN: I wrote that.

CARL: Just passed it off as my own. [*A beat.*] They loved it.

MARILYN: I guess after being my poetry teacher all these months, you're entitled.

CARL: I'm really here to get you to run off with me.

MARILYN: Playing John Wayne?

CARL: I've always wanted to rescue Marilyn Monroe.

MARILYN: Oh, for heaven sakes, I'm perfectly all right. I wanted you to come by tonight so you could see how successful your student is.

CARL: My students don't usually wind up in government.

MARILYN: All those books you got me to read...the poems I've written for you...our long conversations. How could He resist me after that?

CARL: True love, huh?

MARILYN: This love is going to save the world.

CARL: [*Rolls his eyes mockingly and sits at a table.*] Right now, let's save Carl. I need tea. With brandy in it. [*A beat.*] A samovar?

MARILYN: From an admirer.

CARL: [*Holds up his cup.*] Folk Art?

MARILYN: Another admirer.

CARL: Cups with two ears?

MARILYN: No two ears are the same.

CARL: [*A beat as he watches her put the cup under the samovar spout.*] Don't tell me you're going to pour?

[*She abruptly puts the cup down without pouring tea in it and gets a silver shaker.*]

CARL: [*Looking around.*] Five phones?

MARILYN: I have fans, you know. [*She holds up the cocktail shaker.*] Do you want sugar ... milk ... ?

CARL: Brandy.

MARILYN: All I got is a shaker of Daiquiris.

CARL: Shaker on in.

MARILYN: One lump or two?

CARL: The usual.

[MARILYN *pours the daiquiri into his cup and then she adds a quick flip of tea from the samovar and stirs.*]

MARILYN: [*Pours daiquiris into her own cup and stirs.*] I measure my life in boozy spoons.

CARL: "In the room the women come and go ..."

MARILYN: "... speaking of Michelangelo." [*She drinks the contents of her cup.*]

CARL: So you're still on T. S. Eliot?

MARILYN: I'm not still on Eliot. Eliot's still on me.

CARL: You remembered.

MARILYN: When Eliot finishes a poem, he's just another reader. [*A beat.*] After a man is elected, he's just another voter.

CARL: And after a lover loves?

MARILYN: That's the way I feel about my movies. When I looked at

Let's Make Love the other night while I was waiting around for somebody...

CARL: You seem to be waiting around for people these days.

MARILYN: I didn't know who the girl was in that movie.

CARL: [*Singing to the tune of "Billy Boy" as he strums the guitar.*]
Don't you want to be a poet
Norma Jean, Norma Jean?
Don't you want to leave the rot
charmin Norma?
It wouldn't be a thrill
to sell out for caviar and dill
you're a smart girl who oughta leave the lo...t.

MARILYN: Are you making a statement about my acting?

CARL: [*He looks at her and smiles.*] You're my golden sun.

[*A beat as she looks curiously at him.*]

CARL: Colette's mother always said that to her.

MARILYN: I have to admit, nobody's ever loved me like a mother. Especially not my mother. [*A beat.*] You know, Yves Montand is flat footed.

CARL: No, I didn't know that.

MARILYN: He has a hell of a time buying shoes.

CARL: I didn't know that.

MARILYN: Sometimes I walk round and round in this room just like in Van Gogh's prison pictures. [*A beat.*] I've only waited for two people in my life. Him... and Abe. [*A beat.*] You're my Abraham Lincoln.

CARL: I'll warn you, I'm not too old fashioned when it comes to women.

MARILYN: Neither was Lincoln.

CARL: You're the first person who understands that.

MARILYN: I could have been his wife.

CARL: Hidden away in the White House? You could have been him.

MARILYN: They both had blisters on their eyes. From crying when little Willie died.

CARL: Did you read that in my book?

MARILYN: In mine. I've lost children.

CARL: We've all lost children.

MARILYN: Can you believe She bleaches her arm hairs? [*A beat.*] Was she wearing a silly pill box?

CARL: Isn't pill box a military installation?

MARILYN: Her hat.

CARL: Looks a little Mao-ist, don't you think?

MARILYN: Did she put her little cultivated hand on yours...while she cooed about your...meter? [*She says "meter" like "Peter."*]

CARL: Wasn't she nice to poor old Frost? When he lost his way at the Inauguration...his papers flying all around his head?

MARILYN: Have more tea.

CARL: No thanks.

MARILYN: You're being petulant.

CARL: A new vocabulary word. From Mr. Wonderful?

MARILYN: Actually, I picked it up from Yves Montand.

CARL: No flat language he...

MARILYN: Don't tell me you're jealous of Yves Montand, too?

CARL: I'm jealous of everybody.

MARILYN: Are you trying to be theatrical to show the error in being theatrical?

CARL: Marilyn...oh, Marilyn, I'm trying very hard not to fall in love with you.

MARILYN: That's not much of a compliment.

CARL: Do you want a compliment?

MARILYN: Try one.

CARL: You're as real to me as Lincoln.

MARILYN: What else?

CARL: It's your turn.

MARILYN: I like your hair.

CARL: I like yours.

MARILYN: They're putting our mops all over the covers of books and magazines.

CARL: The public always imitates what we find the most silly about ourselves.

MARILYN: I have only one regret—one more than Piaf who regretted nothing. [*A beat.*] Just once, I want to spread my brains at the same time I spread my thighs.

CARL: What about the literary husband you've left? I would think he did it.

MARILYN: [*Grabs* CARL's *guitar and sings.*]
What does the writer
have under his pen.
ha-wang
ha-wang...

CARL: What about your new love?

MARILYN: He can't do both at the same time.

CARL: Pretty scary for a man to take on different ends of a woman all at once.

MARILYN: All my husbands hang pictures of me on the wall—groin high.

CARL: And I wouldn't?

MARILYN: You'd have my little verses attached.

CARL: Never mind. I'm old enough to be your grandfather.

MARILYN: That excites me.

CARL: Time is on the side of my pen.

MARILYN: Your poems excite me.

CARL: But I tend goats.

MARILYN: [*Fondly.*] Yah.

CARL: I smell of fly repellent, pine tar, Lysol. I wear hoof trimmers in my back pocket.

MARILYN: You have a wife.

CARL: My wife has me.

MARILYN: Do you know why I like you?

CARL: I'm photographed all the time.

MARILYN: We both have dirt under our fingernails. [*Looking at her fingernails.*] The orphanage still clings to its roots.

CARL: The family's an orphan.

MARILYN: But only one person can serve the time.

CARL: When I was a kid, I had to clean all the manure from the shed. There were bells on the handle of my shovel. When the bells didn't ring, my father ran out and boxed my ears. [*A beat.*] I got a love of music that way.

MARILYN: There were no bells on my mops and pails. You know more than anybody—I'm boring.

CARL: America doesn't think so.

MARILYN: You mean fans?

CARL: I have fans, too. They aren't so bad.

MARILYN: But you know what they want.

CARL: Not my body parts.

MARILYN: You can have the hidden me.

CARL: Joe wouldn't like it.

MARILYN: Joe? Joe! You and your love of baseball.

CARL: It's the poet's game. You can do a lot of writing between innings.

MARILYN: Joe gets so bored in the winter.

CARL: Winding up a pitch is just as fine a thing as sliding in for a rime. And don't forget Hemingway.

MARILYN: "I'd like to take the great DiMaggio fishing. They say his father's a fisherman."

CARL: *The Old Man and the Sea.*

MARILYN: Joe would rather fish around in my mouth. [*Opens her mouth.*] Under all these caps, I'm Dracula. [*A beat.*] The man who was the kindest to me was a dentist.

CARL: Goats never disappoint me, either.

MARILYN: He had his hands in my mouth. Up to his knuckles. Yet he never... never... enjoyed it. [*A beat.*] Some of the caps come out. See if you can find them.

CARL: Goats are the poor man's cow.

MARILYN: That impresses me.

CARL: Their teats don't have to be large.

MARILYN: Well, aren't they lucky. [*A beat.*] Go on. Find the ones that move.

CARL: You can get a quart of milk a day if you're careful. [*He puts two fingers in her mouth.*]

MARILYN: Feels good.

CARL: Your teeth are solid. [*He takes his fingers away.*] What did the good dentist say when he first looked into the mouth of Marilyn Monroe?

MARILYN: He... gasped. Like this. [*She makes a sigh of disgust.*]

CARL: Over a few cavities?

MARILYN: There was the stench.

CARL: [*He puts two fingers from both his hands and opens her mouth.*] Your tongue was covered with sticky film. Bacteria lined the root ends. Enamel, the hardest substance made by the body, was tortured by scum. Rancid food and acids sheathed the nodes and flaps of tissue. You opened to him—acid, water, dirty enzymes, filthy cell hairs, sticky mucus. [*He lets her mouth close.*]

MARILYN: He hadn't expected it. When I knew him better, he said the smell was as foul as dead bodies dragged into the Los Angeles Morgue where he worked as a student.

CARL: When he cleaned away all the foul, he said: "Now your lovers can kiss you."

MARILYN: And I said . . . "now I have to let them."

CARL: There's a scar on your neck.

MARILYN: It's from nobody famous. [*A beat.*] I'm really trying not to be so affectionate toward scripts.

CARL: When I start to write, I bring on to the page all my friends, my loves, my hates. Then I get absorbed and slowly these people and things leave. And then even I leave. [*A beat.*] There's a scar on your wrist.

MARILYN: From somebody famous. [*A beat.*] I love the way you pull that off—especially in your poem, *Chicago.*

CARL: You really do read me.

MARILYN: I read you 'cause your city doesn't look up my dress.

CARL: Oh, it looks up your dress, all right.

MARILYN: And because you write about ordinary people.

CARL: There are no ordinary people.

MARILYN: How do you do it?

CARL: The way you say . . . "Joe."

MARILYN: [*Says steamily.*] Joe . . . Joe.

CARL: There. See what you've written.

MARILYN: The audience has to discover the thing you hold back. The audience has to take away the mystery. [*A beat.*] Joe . . . no . . .

CARL: Be your own enemy. Fight against what's wrong in your art.

MARILYN: I think so much about the imaginary characters I play—their problems, their joys—that I doubt the living.

CARL: Neither one of us ever wanted to be real people. [*A beat.*] Please, let your hair down.

MARILYN: He prefers a twist.

CARL: Well, that's what counts.

MARILYN: [*Takes out her hair pins and lets her hair fall down.*] He likes it this way in bed.

CARL: Is the bed good?

MARILYN: In what way?

CARL: All the way.

MARILYN: [*She sits on the bed.*] He's efficient.

CARL: Can't be too much fun for you.

MARILYN: He's decisive.

CARL: Do you respond likewise?

MARILYN: Carl, don't make fun of me.

CARL: You're making fun of you.

MARILYN: This affects the world.

CARL: Weren't Picasso's guitars more intense than his people?

MARILYN: I'm talking about the President of the United States.

CARL: Just met him. [*A beat.*] Come away with me. Tonight.

[*A silent beat.*]

MARILYN: I'm helping Him.

CARL: He's using you.

MARILYN: I'm using Him.

CARL: So, now you're the woman behind the throne?

MARILYN: The woman beside the throne.

CARL: A woman's already there, Marilyn.

MARILYN: He doesn't love her.

CARL: He loves you?

MARILYN: At first, He wanted other women when he had me. Usually He likes more than one of us at the same time.

CARL: [*Strums his guitar and chant-sings.*]
Little lusts have lesser lusts
upon their groins to urge them;
lesser lusts have smaller lusts
and so ad infinitum.

MARILYN: Don't make fun. Lust is expensive.

CARL: You only think that 'cause you give it away. [*He takes a coin from his pocket.*] A penny can buy you anything.

MARILYN: [*Takes the penny.*] So . . . you learned to love Lincoln from a penny, too.

CARL: Wild mountain goats are able to stand on a space no bigger than that. [*He takes the penny back and holds it out.*]

MARILYN: Do you think we could ever fill a space so big?

CARL: Sure. [*A beat.*] Cling to me. Like Darwin on the back of those huge tortoises in the Galapagos islands.

[CARL *moves her to his back. She gets on his back and he takes her piggy-back around the room.*]

MARILYN: [*Singing on his back to the tune of "Billy Boy."*]
Is a lady on your back
farmer Carl, farmer Carl?
Is a lady on your back
far . . . mer Ca . . . rl?

CARL: [*Singing.*] There's a lassie on my chassie
trying hard to get my sassy . . .

[CARL *and* MARILYN *fall happily onto the bed.*]

CARL: My age. My idiotic poetic age. [*A beat.*] Do you still put your panties in the refrigerator?

MARILYN: Keeps them cool in the summertime.

CARL: I saw *The Seven Year Itch*.

MARILYN: Oh, you read me, too.

CARL: Are the "cool" panties on, now?

MARILYN: I hate it when you talk like that.

CARL: You mean like a man?

MARILYN: I mean like a fan.

CARL: There. We've rimed together. And that's all I ever wanted.

MARILYN: [*She pulls away from him and stands.*] Do you think you're the only one who resists me? [*A beat.*] Think this lamp lusts after me? [*She throws the lamp on the floor.*] Think this table wants me in bed? [*She throws the end-table against the wall.*] See those props? I've learned about orphans from them. [*A beat.*] I'd look outside . . . longing . . . licking the window pane.

CARL: You watched the bugs on the floor. Wondering if you could be that strong.

MARILYN: They kept bright lights on all night at the orphanage. My shadow was a giant against the wall. I couldn't believe it was me.

CARL: You were already on the screen.

MARILYN: I unbuttoned dreaming.

CARL: The good disadvantage.

MARILYN: When I was twelve and got my first period, I screamed to the walls: I'm learning to think.

CARL: Thinking starts the blood. [*A beat.*] I began to bleed playing the strings on my first guitar.

MARILYN: It's about my time of the month . . . my blood is beginning to run.

CARL: It's your attachment to common life.

MARILYN: Yes, I can spot the common orphan anywhere.

CARL: Turn me loose in a field, and I can find a goat.

MARILYN: I used to go to Times Square. Stand against a building. And look for orphans. Cheaters. Trying to pass themselves off. Trying to act like they had plenty of room growing up. When I know the beds in any orphanage are so close together you can't walk between them. So close together you can stir them with a stick. Beds with metal bars like a circus cage. I stood in those beds to change. Clothes hang a different way on me. [*A beat.*] Of all the painters you've shown me, it's Rembrandt I like best. His little mangy dogs. Those lost dogs he puts on his canvas for the common people. Stray dogs follow orphans—skulking after little girls with dirty hair . . . little girls in eyes filmed with red haw like a hunting dog. [*A beat.*] I ate dried apples for breakfast, dried apples for lunch. And drank a quart of water and swelled for dinner.

CARL: My first poems were naming horses. Purple Rose. Timber Line. Road Salt. Smartweed. My first guitar was made from a big fat seed box and some fence wire. My art came from the same place as the hoe. How more alike can we be?

MARILYN: I had long curls that bounced around like sea anemones.

CARL: In the Orphanage?

MARILYN: Yes.

CARL: They cut them off.

MARILYN: Yes.

CARL: You screamed.

MARILYN: I could see my bald shadow on the wall.

CARL: You kept the curly scraps.

MARILYN: Oh, yes. And sewed them into my pillow.

CARL: Don't regret hair.

MARILYN: Those little curls could think for themselves without any regard for my head.

CARL: Be thankful their martyrdom is over.

MARILYN: Have you got a knife?

CARL: I always carry one for peeling apples.

MARILYN: Like Frost?

CARL: You're still with Eliot, remember?

MARILYN: Give me the knife.

CARL: Take back Frost.

MARILYN: You mean—take back both of him?

CARL: One will do.

MARILYN: A person who can sing is two people. Give me the knife.

CARL: I'm the one who has to think of endings.

MARILYN: I'm dreaming in Ibsen. I'm dreaming in Proust.

CARL: I can't bear the fact that other people write.

MARILYN: Acting can be as satisfying as murder.

CARL: It's that long silence of the blank white sheet of paper that hates life and laughter. I fear its mysterious forces breathing against my hand.

MARILYN: Give me the knife.

CARL: My mother cut out all my shirts with a butcher knife.

MARILYN: Your mother was large, with feet as big as footballs.

CARL: I twisted myself some homemade spurs out of piano wire. I wrote poetry on a piece of paper nailed on the back of my walking cultivator.

MARILYN: You were Zola. Using two quarts of ink a year.

CARL: I had cramps in my hands from cheese making.

MARILYN: Give me the knife.

CARL: I take time paring an apple. That's real writing.

[CARL *takes the penknife from his back pocket and slowly hands it to* MARILYN. *She takes the knife and begins stabbing a pillow on the bed and bright yellow brassy feathers pop out of the pillow and fall everywhere.*]

MARILYN: My curls. From the orphanage. [*She looks down at the feathers and begins to sort tenderly through the feathers.*] All my sweet lost children. You little raw pulps that were my babies. I love every one of you. [*Abruptly.*] Isn't well made fiction wonderful?

CARL: Fiction holds the world together. [CARL *gets his guitar and sings.*]
On top of sweet Marilyn
all covered with glitter,
she keeps right on singing
about her life's litter.

MARILYN: [*Singing.*] Her voice is so mournful...

CARL: [*Singing.*] ...with sobs and with tears...

MARILYN: [*Singing.*] Marilyn's been cashing in on the orphanage...

CARL: [*Singing.*] ...for the past 36 years.

CARL & MARILYN: [*Singing.*] On top of ole Carl
all covered with bells...

CARL: [*Singing.*] He's been bagging his poverty...

MARILYN: [*Singing.*] Cause poverty sells.

[*They embrace, laughing.*
MARILYN *suddenly pulls away from* CARL.]

MARILYN: You know he's deformed.

CARL: Your President?

MARILYN: Yes.

CARL: What about all the swimming and football games?

MARILYN: Those things don't happen as often as you think.

CARL: Are you trying to enlist my sympathy?

MARILYN: He hates sympathy.

CARL: Even from you?

MARILYN: Daily enemas. Salt water boils. Migraines. He vomits all the time from the pain.

CARL: It must have been a big help having once been married to a baseball player.

MARILYN: Joe always walks around with his elbow in a bucket of ice.

CARL: All his sprained ankles . . . sore arms . . .

MARILYN: I like the look of pain. It's real.

CARL: And your new Mr. Wonderful has all that glamorous agony.

MARILYN: He feels so awful, half the time he won't even let me touch him.

CARL: How do you manage that?

MARILYN: I try to touch him when he's not paying attention.

CARL: I can't imagine a man not paying attention.

MARILYN: When he's . . . deep in conversation.

CARL: So he does talk to you?

MARILYN: He told me to put a lump of sugar behind my teeth and drink tea through it, Russian style.

CARL: Affairs of State.

MARILYN: I'm reading a book on diseases of the mouth.

CARL: For all the times he's impotent?

MARILYN: If sex were successful 99.9 percent of the time, there would still be 2 limp dicks every day. [*A beat.*] Believe me, he asks my opinion on things.

CARL: Castro?

MARILYN: I told him to have a list ready of some good Cuban doctors living in Miami.

CARL: In case he bombed the hell out of a lot of Cuban civilians.

MARILYN: It would be humane.

CARL: Sounds like hard-core strategy to me.

MARILYN: Just the old battle between grace and liberty, between St. Augustine and St. Thomas.

CARL: Maybe you ought to read more poems and less religion. Your man is a poet, after all. Short phrases. Alliteration. "We stand in a new Frontier—Frontier of perils, promises...

MARILYN: I've got Byron.

CARL: Was that his choice?

MARILYN: It was your choice. Our first lunch. At the Algonquin. Remember? You said you admired a poet who fought for his convictions.

CARL: Did you read Byron right after our lunch?

MARILYN: War didn't interest me.

CARL: You hadn't been politicized then?

[*A beat.*]

CARL: [*Cont'd.*] What are these terrible rumors? These ugly insinuations? [*A beat.*] Let me take you away from here.

MARILYN: You'd take me away from my best role.

[*The phone rings. She answers the phone.*]

MARILYN: [*Into the phone.*] Hello... [*A beat.*] It's arrived? Good. Bring it upstairs. I don't want to be disturbed; just leave it by the door. Thanks.

CARL: How long are you planning to stay in Washington?

MARILYN: As long as he wants me.

CARL: So you're making a little nest here?

MARILYN: That's a cliché, isn't it?

CARL: Aren't you living one?

MARILYN: Damnit, Carl, I'm trying to be my own actress.

CARL: Very profound.

MARILYN: I'm not one Marilyn Monroe all the time.

CARL: Maybe one is all he wants.

MARILYN: Then acting will be my oldest profession.

[*A beat.*]

CARL: He's no Lincoln, for godsakes.

MARILYN: I know . . . He's not that thin.

CARL: A little paunch, is it?

MARILYN: He loves Milky Ways.

CARL: Cosmic, even when he eats?

MARILYN: He hides them in the dresser under his socks.

CARL: In the Chester Arthur Chester Drawers?

MARILYN: His wife has him on a diet all the time.

CARL: And you wouldn't?

MARILYN: Why would I want to do that?

CARL: You'd be responsible for him, wouldn't you?

MARILYN: He's got Secret Service men for that.

CARL: You'd turn over control to strangers?

MARILYN: Of course it's true—he can't afford any extra weight on his back. I told him, if I wanted to assassinate him, I'd aim a rifle full of heavy duty chocolate at his head.

CARL: You told him that?

MARILYN: I told him that and he said . . . never tell my enemies.

CARL: And are there enemies out there who want to get him?

MARILYN: Everybody in the world loves our Man. *Lass' sie nach Berlin kommen!*

CARL: Wrong country.

MARILYN: Right fanaticism.

CARL: You do have potential for politics.

[*She hears a thud by the door and goes to open it. There is a rocking chair covered with brown butcher paper. She pulls it inside the room and shuts the door. She excitedly unwraps the package to reveal a sturdy wooden rocking chair.*]

CARL: His?

MARILYN: A very good imitation.

CARL: Like Monet in those pink plastic frames at the dimestore,

MARILYN: Do you go to dimestores?

CARL: You see the best paintings there.

MARILYN: I never thought of the Mona Lisa as great. 'Cause it was always on chocolate boxes when I was a kid. Then when I grew up and saw it at the Louvre in Paris...I said, "What do you know. I've been gobbling up art all this time."

CARL: [*Touching the rocking chair.*] I've seen the original.

MARILYN: I guess I can take it off my income tax.

[*A silent beat. Then* CARL *puts the paper back over the rocking chair.*]

CARL: I came here to take you home.

MARILYN: If I had a home, Carl, you could take me there.

CARL: Stay with us on the farm.

MARILYN: Forever?

CARL: There's that Italian director who wants you for his next film in a couple of months.

MARILYN: I don't speak Italian.

CARL: You don't have to.

MARILYN: Who could dub my voice?

CARL: Rome.

MARILYN: Be serious.

CARL: We'll feed you goat cheese for two months. Then put you on a plane for Italy. You'll cross the ocean at night and see the Great Dipper and the Little Bear outside your oval window. All the stars and the rest of the Orion will swirl around you, a harvest of glittering new fans.

MARILYN: But you'll be down on the ground—silent and far away from me.

CARL: And lamenting my age.

[*A silent beat.*]

MARILYN: I can't leave Washington. [*She takes the paper off the rocking chair.*]

CARL: I'm going back to Illinois on the train. At 5 A.M. [*A beat.*] Come with me. We'll ride together through our America. Grain dust and acres of yellow wheat blowing at our backs. We'll stick our heads out the window and let our famous hair stream out behind us. [*A beat.*] We need the sympathy of mountain peaks and bluff grass. [*A beat.*] We'll reach out and touch rocks as red as new bricks. Eat wild grapes right from the vine. American dreamers—that's us. Come with me. Let's sing to the wild artichokes and bull thistles. Let's wave at the ponds and sloughs. Smell the moss roses. Wish on the prairie mud. American Dreamers. It's what we do best.

[*A silent beat.*]

MARILYN: I can't.

CARL: Why not?

MARILYN: He needs me.

CARL: So do I? Who will keep me honest?

MARILYN: Who will keep him honest?

CARL: You're in a "B" movie, my friend.

MARILYN: He has a file-cabinet marked "lies."

CARL: Have you given up poetic reasoning?

[*A beat. She goes to the rocking chair, picks it up, and puts it on the center of the bed.*]

MARILYN: "Sir Lancelot... thou are the goodlyest person that ever came among knights..."

CARL: Thomas Malory.

MARILYN: You gave him to me.

CARL: Undercover work for Mr. President is not what I call poetry.

MARILYN: I call Mr. President...Doc.

CARL: As in Papa Doc?

MARILYN: As in "lover Doc."

CARL: His divinity ails him.

MARILYN: Just like my divinity ails me. [*A beat.*] You can't expect him to get ordinary relief.

CARL: Are you putting the scrotum around the man?

MARILYN: Once...before we did it in his official bedroom...he took a short swim. I sat at one end of the White House Pool. And every time he swam down to me, he grabbed a breast.

CARL: Presidential foreplay. Ask not what your breasts can do for you; ask what your breasts can do for your country.

MARILYN: Of course I was holding his daiquiri.

CARL: Did you say anything through this foreplay?

MARILYN: Yes. But I had to time myself. I'd go: "Why do we have Jupiter missiles in Turkey?" Lap one. Breast one. "Those missiles are useless and out of date." Lap two. Breast two. "How can we make demands on Cuba with stuff like that?" Lap three. Both breasts.

CARL: How do you know about Turkey?

MARILYN: I've got a loyal fan in Istanbul.

CARL: Do you ever get any answers beside this pool?

MARILYN: No. But talking politics is exciting.

CARL: Dirty.

MARILYN: Yah.

CARL: And how is the loving after a swim?

MARILYN: Pro forma.

CARL: That's all?

MARILYN: Church songs came over the orphanage wall. I'm his religion.

CARL: I believe his mother already gave him one.

MARILYN: Mom wears a large Crucifix in her belt. Like a missionary.

CARL: She walks among Pagans.

MARILYN: When the pain gets bad, he curses God. If he were an atheist, he couldn't. So, his Mother can take credit for that.

CARL: And you? What do you take credit for?

MARILYN: When he's at the peak of his pleasure, he forgets his back pain. Being in me is like being in Church. Incense... the chalice held on high... two Hosts on the paten... *Deo Gracias*... final calm. I assure you, if he could screw me all the time, he wouldn't have to go to Mass.

CARL: Well, you've done wonders for Paula and me.

MARILYN: Really?

CARL: You've sparked my old garden tools.

MARILYN: Oh, tell me.

CARL: I put her down like a fat fragrant peony. The bed is chocolaty fudge dirt. She bucks and weaves. I'm a sun-hot trellis and, oh, what pollination we do make.

[*A silent beat.*]

MARILYN: I did all that?

CARL: Yep.

MARILYN: Sounds almost as good as what Doc and I call our summits.

CARL: Summits?

MARILYN: I gulp down a lot of pills. We don't have much time to make out—before I get comatose. Soon as he pulls out of me, he puts his finger down my throat and forces everything up.

CARL: The way he gestures... jabbing the air with one forefinger. Now I know where that finger's been.

MARILYN: He said he learned how to deal with international crises from me. [*A beat.*] Of course...the longer we wait...the more "Crisis." He likes to feel my pulse. A reminder that time is measured. In a dark way. If he doesn't vomit me, the anonymous constancy of my heart beats will turn into silence and blindness.

CARL: Is this exciting for you?

MARILYN: I never climax, if that's what you mean.

CARL: Why not?

MARILYN: He'd view that as retaliation.

[*Silent beat. Suddenly, the saucer-sized disc over her bed beings to sputter and glow in sparks of yellow.*]

CARL: What in the world is that?

MARILYN: A false alarm. [*A beat.*] When he enters the bedroom up above mine, it turns red. Then I know he'll be here in twenty minutes.

CARL: I suppose he swings down on a rope to your room like Tarzan.

[CARL *goes to look at the disk as it sputters.*]

MARILYN: Once it went bonkers like that when we were making love.

CARL: Some monster trying to bless you, no doubt. [*He looks at the trailing wire. He follows a fine wire that goes to the window and outside the window and upward. He opens the window to look at the wire going up.*]

MARILYN: Don't open the window. You'll let all the hot air come in. It's bad for Doc's sinuses.

[CARL *closes the window. He takes a small pocket wrench out of his tux pocket and goes to the sputtering disk. He tinkers. Then he gives a solid rap to the disk with his wrench. The disc stops sputtering.*]

MARILYN: How did you fix it?

CARL: [*Shaking wrench at her.*] Unlike you, I retaliate.

[*A silent beat as she stares at him.*]

CARL: Somebody in Chicago told me a pretty harsh rumor about your "man."

MARILYN: Who?

CARL: A real estate agent with one foot in Las Vegas. His kid is studying poetry at the University of Chicago. All three of us had lunch at Walgreens Drugstore on State Street last week.

MARILYN: Walgreens?

CARL: He takes my grass roots seriously.

MARILYN: So, what did he tell you?

CARL: Your "Doc" is hooked up with the Mafia.

MARILYN: Is that suppose to shock me?

CARL: And when a person implicates him . . . that person disappears.

MARILYN: You ought to eat in better places.

CARL: I had to recite two narrative poems and a couplet over the oilcloth counter just to get that lunch paid for.

MARILYN: Are you still mooching free meals?

CARL: I don't enjoy my food when I have to pay for it.

MARILYN: What does some salesman in remote Chicago know about anything.

CARL: The 2nd City.

MARILYN: You're prejudiced.

CARL: When it comes to Chicago, it's good business for me to be prejudiced.

MARILYN: I wish you'd never written that poem.

CARL: If you're in search of thugs, consult Milton.

MARILYN: I consult Shakespeare. The White House copy.

CARL: I hate Shakespeare.

MARILYN: You and Tolstoy. Mad cause the Bard didn't make heroes out of farmers.

CARL: Are you making heroes out of the Mafia?

MARILYN: They're just another political party.

CARL: I don't think it's legal for any party to bump off annoying constituents.

MARILYN: Is that what the salesman in remote Chicago is saying?

CARL: Ever read Hans Andersen's "Little Mermaid?" For love . . . she exchanged her fish tail for a woman's legs. Then found herself walking on needles and burning coals.

MARILYN: [*Picks up a books and extends it toward him.*] I stick to Clausewitz.

CARL: [*Takes book and read the title.*] Philosophy of War. [*A beat.*] The White House copy?

MARILYN: 20th Century Fox's copy.

[*One of the phone rings.* MARILYN *picks it up.*]

MARILYN: [*Into phone.*] 508 . . . Look, I'm busy. Carl's here. You know all about him. Carl Sandburg. I told you last week, this is the night he's reading for the U. S. Senators and then he was coming by the hotel to see me and I don't have too much time with him 'cause I'm on call and pretty soon I'll have to . . . yes . . . but . . . I know you're busy, too. But . . . yes . . . yes . . . oh, ok.
[*She hands the phone to* CARL.] He wants to speak to you.

CARL: Who?

MARILYN: Nikita. [*Silent pause.*] Khrushchev.

[*As* CARL *is talking to Nikita,* MARILYN *goes to the closet and rolls out a large world map with pins. She takes a pin from the margin of the map and holds it as she studies the map.*]

CARL: [*Into phone.*] Sandburg. [*Listening.*] Yes, I wrote that . . . yes, I wrote that, too. I didn't know you were fond of poetry . . . naturally I realize the great poets are Russian—like Pushkin . . . you write poetry? [*Listening to Khrushchev read his original poem.*] Hmmmmmmmm, good cadence. Good riming. A few purple passages on the last part, Nikita. [*Listening.*] No, that's not capitalistic propaganda. "Purple mountains majesty" is capitalistic propaganda. Yes . . . yes . . . I read Frost. And Robert Service. [*Listening.*] Oh, you must mean Harriet Monroe? . . . You mean Marilyn Monroe. "When Lincoln makes love/there's only bread." . . . yes, of course, I'm quite familiar with that poem. You quoted it at the Soviet Trade Exhibition in Havana in '61? It makes you determined to have good relations with the U.S.

Well, that's the power of poetry. I'll give you back to the poetess.

MARILYN: [*Into the phone.*] My Nikita Mariquita. When will I see you again? Not for a whole month? Yes...yes...of course I'm disappointed...but you're going to Cuba, right? Yes...yes...I know you'll make time for me. Yes, I'm drinking tea from it right now. You stole it from Gromyko? Well, it's beautiful. Yes...yes, I've got the papers. Right here. [*She points to under the mattress for* CARL *to get them, but he looks under the bed instead.* CARL *comes out from under the bed with two hip waders which he holds up against him.*] Yes...yes, you'll send a courier for them? Right. I understand. They'll be ready. [*She motions* CARL *to look under the mattress. He abruptly drops the hip-waders on the floor. He pulls out a brown envelope from under the mattress and holds it out to her.*] I'm holding them right now. Of course I'll be careful. I'm not going to let anybody intercept them. Keep your shoes on, Nicky. [*She hangs up. Happily slapping at the rocking chair.*] Dah!

[*She picks up the hip-waders and puts them sexily up against her thighs as she smiles and parades in front of the rocking chair. Then she throws the hip waders back under the bed.*]

CARL: Giving away a few secrets in this envelope?

MARILYN: [*She goes back to looking at the world map still holding the pin.*] Look for yourself. I'll tell you one thing, I'll never play pinball with Nicky again. He always puts the machine on top of his shoes and uses his belly to win a game. Now, do you think that's fair?

CARL: [*Looking at the brown envelope hesitantly.*] I don't know if I want to see this.

MARILYN: Afraid to get involved?

CARL: Afraid to be a traitor.

MARILYN: You think I'm a traitor?

CARL: Giving Nikita information that your love-Doc screams out when he arches in passion?

MARILYN: Doc comes so fast, he wouldn't have time to scream out the first word of a top secret.

[CARL *gingerly opens the envelope slowly.*]

CARL: It's a calendar.

MARILYN: Recognize me?

CARL: [*Flips through calendar pages.*] These are the "papers" for Nikita!

MARILYN: You'll find a courier envelope in one of those dresser drawers—under my drawers.

[*She sticks the map pin saying "Moscow" on the world map.*
CARL goes to the map.]

MARILYN: I have "calendars" where all these pins are.

[*The phone rings.* MARILYN *picks it up.*]

MARILYN: [*Into phone.*] 508. Yes. Speaking. I got the cups. I'm drinking out of them right now. [*She motions* CARL *to give her the cup.*] How's Raul? Good. I'm glad you both like it. I'm sending the same "papers" to Nikita...I'm sorry Esso and Texaco pulled out of your country. We can talk about that when I see you. Yes...I'm looking forward to our visit. I want to see everything on your beautiful island. See you then. Adios, Fidel. [*She hangs up and slaps the rocking chair saying "ole!"*]

[*As* MARILYN *is speaking,* CARL *opens the dresser drawer and he picks up an official envelope with Russian lettering on it. A pair of black lace panties are stuck to the envelope.*]

CARL: Castro?

MARILYN: [*Holds up cup and points to "C."*] He says the "C" isn't for Castro. It stands for "Communism."

CARL: I believe Hoover calls it "Commonism."

MARILYN: I don't know why Doc doesn't get rid of him. Hoover can't even pronounce things right.

CARL: Maybe because your Doc is on the Index.

MARILYN: Everybody's on the Index. If they started rounding up all Hoover's suspicious people, you'd need Madison Square Garden to hold them.

[CARL *puts the calendar in the courier envelope and puts the panties back in the drawer.*]

MARILYN: Oh, what the hell. Nicky likes my poetry. [MARILYN *goes to the dresser and takes the panties back out and puts them in the courier envelope with the calendar, licks the envelope, and then lifts off the mirror above the dresser and pulls down a mailbox lid and drops the courier envelope down the chute.*]

CARL: Your own Russian mailbox?

MARILYN: Ambassador Dobrynin is on the first floor.

[MARILYN *puts the mirror back on the wall above the dresser. She looks in the mirror.*]

MARILYN: I look like hell.

CARL: [*He makes a foot gesture at the space under the bed.*] Hip waders?

MARILYN: You know how water sports turn him on. [*A beat.*] I'm afraid I got some bad news for Doc tonight. I keep hearing from Poco that some missiles are going up in San Cristobal.

CARL: Surely he knows.

MARILYN: Doc wants Castro out. But, he thinks Castro can't last. I know better. Fidel can last. [*A beat.*] I'll send a plane to Cuba to take some high altitude pictures.

CARL: Just remember: No bird soars too high ... if it soars with its own wings.

[*Phone rings.*]

MARILYN: You answer it.

[CARL *hesitates.*]

MARILYN: Go on.

[MARILYN *goes to the rocking chair on the bed, takes it off and puts it on the floor. She sits in it.*]

CARL: [*Into phone.*] Monroe. [*He listens.*] Just a minute please. [*Handing her the phone.*] It's George Bundy.

MARILYN: Take a message.

[CARL *stares at* MARILYN *helplessly as she continues to stare at the rocking chair.*]

CARL: [*To* MARILYN.] The Presidential Assistant for National Security.

[MARILYN *rocks without answering.*]

CARL: [*Into phone.*] Miss Monroe has her hands full right now. Can I relay a message to her? [*Listens. To* MARILYN.] He wants your opinion on a possible Denfense Condition #2.

MARILYN: I have to talk to Sweeney. Tactical Air Command. I'll call him back tomorrow.

CARL: She needs another day. [*Listens.*] Thank you. [*He hangs up.*] He hasn't received the "films."

[*She points under the mattress for* CARL *to get another calendar which he does and then he automatically gets a brown envelope from the drawer.*]

CARL: You'd think he could get his own.

MARILYN: They're scarce. [*A beat.*] Mail it behind the Picasso.

[CARL *goes to the painting and moves it aside. He pulls down a mail-box lid and puts in the brown envelope.*]

MARILYN: I'm trying to invent a new position. [*She stands and looks at the rocking chair. Then she motions to* CARL *to sit in the rocking chair.*] Sit.

[CARL *sits in the rocking chair.*]

MARILYN: Sit tall.

[CARL *sits tall.*
    She straddles him on the rocking chair, one leg on each side, facing him.]

MARILYN: Nope. Too much pressure on his piriformis muscles.

[*She stands. A beat. Then she moves* CARL's *legs apart and sits between his legs, her back to him.*]

MARILYN: Too heavy on his lumbar curve.

[*She stands. She now sits, straddling the arms of the rocking chair, one leg over each arm as she faces him.*]

MARILYN: I've decided on something called the Sacral Rock. [*A beat.*] Now ... just tip over to the left.

[*She gently helps* CARL *tip to the left, all the way over so that she and the rocking chair and* CARL *go over on one side.*]

MARILYN: Keep your back up against the slats. Rock...rock...

[*They fumble, roll around, and end up laughing and flinging themselves on their back looking at the ceiling. After a beat, all five phones ring. Marilyn gets up, gathers all the phone receivers like a bouquet.*]

MARILYN: [*Into all the phones.*] Room 508.
[*She listens to all five telephones by her ear. Into phone #1.*] Commander Thomas Power? [*Listens. Then.*] Five Cuban launcher sites. [*She jerks the plug of this phone out of the wall and tosses the phone aside.*]

[*Into phone #2.*] The C-S-B-F? Oh, the Catholic Service Bureau of Florida. [*Listens. Then.*] Spread the rumor in Cuba that parents will lose the rights of paternity over their kids to the Cuban State. Patria Potestas. [*She yanks the plug of phone #2 out of the wall and tosses the phone aside.*]

[*Into phone #3.*] Mr. Bush? [*Listens. Then.*] They've positioned tactical nuclear battlefield rockets for use against invasion forces. [*She yanks the plug of phone #3 out of the wall and tosses the phone aside.*]

[*Into phone #4.*] Le May? [*Listens. Then.*] Twenty SS-4 M-R-B-Ms able to send megaton-yield warheads as far as Washington. [*She janks the plug of phone #4 out of the wall and tosses the phone aside.*]

[*Into phone #5.*] Third Marine Corps of the Western Hemisphere? [*She listens. Then.*] I want an arsenal of small vessels and yachts—non governmental—ready at all times in the direction of the Cuban coastline. [*She janks out the plug of phone #5 and tosses the phone aside.*]

[*A beat.*] Thank God they all have calendars.

CARL: Doesn't the President do anything himself?

MARILYN: He uses the best people for what he wants done. Smart leadership is dumb leadership.

CARL: You should definitely attend cabinet meetings.

MARILYN: When I walk into a room, personalities change. That's why Doc doesn't attend a lot of important conferences. Even strong people can make recommendations on the basis of what either one of us might want to hear. [*A beat.*] But it torments him that he can't delegate being a Daddy.

CARL: I would think Miss Pill Box does everything.

MARILYN: She can't be Him. [*A beat.*] The power of being a Father is almost more than he can bare. [*A beat.*] Give me my shoe.

CARL: [*He looks in his pockets and brings out a yo-yo.*] I can do "around the world" with my yo-yo.

MARILYN: [*She takes the yo-yo from him and tosses it aside.*] My shoe.

[CARL *takes a shoe off her foot.*]

MARILYN: [*She points to the map with her shoe heel.*] Doc believes in winnable nuclear war.

CARL: Don't say that. I have daughters.

MARILYN: People are always so curious about what it's like to be dead. It's surprising considering how easy it is to imagine. What's it like to be Nikita or Fidel or Doc, that's the real mystery. But to be dead... I only close my eyes and "picture" things and places around me. [*She closes her eyes.*] I picture...the bed as nothing. The closet door...is nothing. The air-conditioner...is nothing. They're all nothing to me, as real as the light picking up their rays. I've fallen into enough darkness to know my mortal limits. [MARILYN *stands and goes to the map and sweeps away the pins on the map with her arm.*]

I can even imagine the world dead. [*A beat.*] Cut a notch in the windpipe of United States...to relax the muscles binding the organ sack. [*She slashes at the United States with her shoe heel and bits of paper fly.*] Slide my index and forefingers under the hide of Moscow, letting out the carnal stink of grass and sage. [*She slashes at Moscow with her shoe and bits of paper from the map fall away.*] Saw down the belly of China, Africa, South America—toward the genitals of Europe. [*She slashes at China, Africa, South America and Europe and bits of paper falls from the map.*] I part the cavity and expose the bloodless gray-green organs of the sea.

CARL: You'd never clean a carcass.

MARILYN: I'll cut out Washington, D.C. The heart. And keep it for myself. [*She wipes off the imaginary blood from her shoe and puts it back on.*]

CARL: Taking only the "heart" is poaching.

MARILYN: You saw *The Misfits?*

CARL: That's why you'd never cut up the world.

MARILYN: The world's not a beautiful wild horse.

CARL: Some of it is.

MARILYN: I'm playing against type.

CARL: Then come to Illinois with me. Play farmer.

MARILYN: I want to play Falstaff. That will convince critics once and for all that I don't have to be Marilyn.

CARL: Be Falstaff in Illinois. [*He goes to the map.*] There's survival in Illinois. Invention and imagination in the rest of the country, too. And in the world. In the darkest tunnel of Pennsylvania, a poem exists. [*He tries to slap the torn paper back on the map.*] If we go into the bowels of Moscow or Africa, we'll find the lines of a Greco face. [*Trying to slap the torn pieces of the map back on.*] The solid black mud of China or South America is Homer, blind but writing away. [*He slaps the torn pieces of the map back on.*]

MARILYN: I want the one performance that will kill all the other ones.

CARL: Come to Illinois. Everybody knows that Illinois is half a day away from half of the USA. We'll sit next to purple corn flowers and wild pink prairie roses without so much as calling them beautiful.

[*Silent beat as she looks at* CARL. *She is shaking her head "no".*]

MARILYN: Help me get ready. [*A beat.*] Help me get ready for Him. [CARL *goes to the end table and opens the drawer and takes out the pill bottles.* CARL *opens the window and throws out all the pill bottles.* MARILYN *calmly watches.*]

MARILYN: [*Cont'd.*] Close the window. All that hot air. He's a sick man. Have some pity.

[CARL *doesn't move.*]

MARILYN: [*Cont'd.*] Most of his childhood was spent in the infirmary of boarding schools. He showed me the pictures. Those infirmaries looked like my orphanage. He slept on musty mattresses. Ate bad food. His parents never came to visit him. Only the books came...Tolstoy...Dickens...Flaubert...Mann. He said he could grasp the head-bars of his sick bed and feel the presence of all the people who had ever slept in his bed before him...telling the short from the tall, the dark from the fair. He could perceive the murmuring of their hearts, the pulse from their weak wrist, the flutter of their breath struggling for air, the movement of listless legs. He could encounter the very character of all those who were sick before him. He could endure their moods: anger, joy, sadness. He knew their hesitancy, their deliberateness. He was experiencing the sensation of the Western Indians who could smell camp fires that they were unable to see. That's how he got to sleep at night—putting his arms over his head and holding on to the metal bed-bars and feeling those invisible suffering souls before him. He could always tell who believed in God and who did not. He knew what part of the country they were from. There were as many cities and towns as philosophies. He knew what food they liked, what flowers they loved, whether they were fond of horses. He said holding on to those bars day after day made him understand human pain and human hope.

[*A beat.* CARL *slowly closes the window. Suddenly, the bulb over the bed begins to beep in red flashes.*]

MARILYN: Help me undress. Then you have to go...it's almost time. [*She gives him a short sweet kiss.* CARL *slowly begins to unbutton her dress. She is facing the audience. He helps her take off the dress as he stands in front of her so we can't see. He throws the dress to the side of the stage. She is standing naked. As* CARL *exits, she takes some pills she has hidden in a light fixture above the bed and she swallows all the pills from the bottle and lies down on the bed. After* CARL *exits, he stands by her closed door outside in the hall.* CARL *leans against the closed door and strums his guitar and talk-sings softly:*]

CARL: Marilyn,
Marilyn,
I'll never go so far

from you
that I won't see
the same old stars
and Venus, too
as you.

Marilyn,
Marilyn,
now my days are long,
long,
if I could sing with you
I wouldn't need a song.

Marilyn,
Marilyn,
I'll never go so far
from you
that I won't see
the same old sun
and moonbeams, too,
as you.

Marilyn,
Marilyn,
now my days are long,
long,
if I could sing with you
I wouldn't need a song.

[*A naval rope ladder falls down from above and clanks beside her window.* MARILYN *groans sluggishly her hand extended out toward the phone near her bed as the lights slowly fade.* CARL, *having finished his song, slowly exits from the hotel hallway.*]

END OF PLAY

John Ford Noonan

WHEN IT COMES EARLY

JOHN FORD NOONAN

John Ford Noonan is a 1989 inductee into the French Society of Composers and Authors. He first came to prominence in 1969 with the highly acclaimed Lincoln Center production of *The Year Boston Won the Pennant*, starring Roy Scheider. It won Mr. Noonan an Obie, a Theatre World and a Pulitzer Prize nomination.

From 1972 to 1977 at Joe Papp's New York Shakespeare Festival, Noonan wrote *Older People* (a Drama Desk Award Winner), *Concerning the Effects of Trimethylchloride*, *Where Do We Go From Here?*, *All the Sad Protestants*, and *Getting Through the Night*. In 1978 his play *The Club Champion's Widow*, with Maureen Stapleton, opened the premiere season of the Robert Lewis Acting Company.

In the 1980's he wrote *A Coupla White Chicks Sitting Around Talking*, which ran for more than 800 performances at the Astor Place Theatre, and *Some Men Need Help* (three months on Broadway). In 1987 Mr. Noonan's *Spanish Confusion*, *Mom Sells Twins For Two Beers*, *Green Mountain Fever* and *Recent Developments In Southern Connecticut* all ran simultaneously in Los Angeles (three of which won Drama-Logue Awards). In 1990, Mr. Noonan wrote his play *Talking Things Over With Chekhov* and also performed the male lead for six months at the Actor's Playhouse. In 1993, the WPA presented his play *Music From Down the Hill*. It was subsequently produced, under the direction of Dorothy Lyman, at the Odyssey Theater in Los Angeles.

Noonan has twice been nominated for an Emmy—in 1984 for an episode of *St. Elsewhere* called "The Women" (which he won) and in 1985 for the television adaptation of *Some Men Need Help*. On screen he has acted in such movies as *Brown Wolf*, *Next Stop, Greenwich Village*; *Heaven Help Us*, *Adventures in Babysitting*, and this past year he appeared in the hit movie *Flirting With Disaster*.

Mr. Noonan's proudest accomplishments to date are: 1) his children: Jesse Sage Noonan, Chris Noonan Howell, Olivia Noonan Howell, and Tracy Noonan Howell, and his secret and favorite fifth, Tom Noonan Nohilly; 2) his acclaim by *Rolling Stone* magazine as "the greatest white boogie dancer in the world"; 3) his being a founding member of the legendary punk band "Pinhead," as well as penning their anthem, *Kill Your Parents, Then We'll Talk*; 4) his being four consecutive times Junior Golf Champion at his home country club in Greenwich, CT. He once shot a sixty-seven followed by an eighty-one; and 5) he loves sentences. His favorite utterance in his whole life was his mother's recent remark, "John, it's never too late to be normal."

CHARACTERS

J.C. WEBRING

MICKEY WEBRING

SETTING: *Bimney Park, Old Greenwich, Connecticut. A park bench USC. DSL a trash can. Neatly manicured grass and cement path winding through. On back of park bench and on front of trash can:* PROPERTY OF THE TOWN OF GREENWICH, CONNECTICUT.

TIME: *Early afternoon, the second week of May, just after 1 P.M.*

Lights up! MICKEY WEBRING *enters first. Early fifties, tall, blond, proud, she wears slacks, sport jacket, and blouse. She carries lunch basket. Puts down basket and crosses back to help husband* J.C. WEBRING. J.C. *is in his mid fifties, wearing large overcoat, gloves, and big floppy hat. He seems to have no hair. It has all been shaved off. He is tall and muscular and yet he moves tentatively and uncertainly.* MICKEY *offers a hand but* J.C. *pushes her away and "shushes" her over to the bench. She laughs and crosses back to the bench, sits, opens lunch basket, takes out red check table cloth and begins to lay out food: two hard-boiled eggs, two sandwiches in a wrapper, fruit in tinfoil and jug of orange-flavored ice tea. Next she takes out plastic forks, napkins, drinking cups, etc. Sets those out, looks up.* J.C. *has gotten half way to bench. She jumps up, her intention to help him but he waves her away again and "shushes" her back to her work.* J.C. *sits. She unfolds a napkin for* J.C. *only he grabs it and slaps it across his lap.* MICKEY *hands* J.C. *a hard-boiled egg. He begins to eat without cracking the shell.* MICKEY *grabs it back and peels it for him.* J.C. *eats egg.* MICKEY *peels own egg, begs us to eat, suddenly laughs.*

MICKEY: It's all changed so little. The pond's still there, so clean, pretty and pure. [*Pointing out over audience.*] The ducks, the swan, that weeping willow, and out there, the little boat house. In the winter they would enclose it, build a fire and all us girls'd help each other lace up. Boy, could I skate!!

J.C.: You were a dandy.

MICKEY: What?

J.C.: Skating along. Flying by in your infamous outfit: white tights, short red skirt, red and white hand warmer, elf cap with the jingle bell on top.

MICKEY: Hold it! How do you—

J.C.: Oh, God! Look!!

MICKEY: Where?

J.C.: Freddy Di Stephano and Archie Manning are fighting over you again.

MICKEY: They were my first two. How do you—

J.C.: They're rolling in the snow. Cathy Nugent runs out onto the ice and grabs at you whizzing by. You scream to a stop. [*"Playing"* CATHY NUGENT.] "Mickey, they're fighting over you again. Do come stop them." [*"Playing"* MICKEY.] "Cathy, it's what I live for, my men killing each other over me."

MICKEY: That's exactly what I said. [*Quoting.*] "It's what I live for, my men killing each other over me."

J.C.: I know.

MICKEY: You weren't there.

J.C.: You told me.

MICKEY: When?

J.C.: The third night of our honeymoon. The Jug End Barn up in the Berkshires. January 8, 1954. We were lying in bed. We heard shouting. We jumped up—looked out—skaters in the moonlight. It's when you told me. [*Laughing.*] Freddy Di Stephano and Archie Manning.

MICKEY: I don't remember telling you.

J.C.: I remember being told. [*J.C. takes* MICKEY'S *hand and kisses it, gently, fondly. Suddenly drops her hand and leaps to his feet.*] Oh God!

MICKEY: What's wrong now?

J.C.: There!

MICKEY: Where?

[*Pointing out over audience, counting something off in distance, whispering "One . . . Two . . . Three."*]

J.C.: The third bench past the big weeping willow?

MICKEY: Yes?

J.C.: That's where your father sat me down and read me the riot act.

MICKEY: J.C., this you're making up.

J.C.: You were away that weekend. Your college roommate Villette Kneeber.

MICKEY: She just got married again. Another dentist.

J.C.: Well, her brother Vincent had been killed on a motorcycle. I took you to the train. Villette lived in Scarsdale.

MICKEY: God, the things you remember!

J.C.: Your dad and I went for a walk. Through the village, up the hill by the railroad and then right over there.

MICKEY: Who spoke first?

J.C.: Who else.

MICKEY: Do his voice!

J.C.: [*"Imitating"* FATHER.] "Now listen here, pal. What are your plans for my gal?!!" [*"Playing"* SELF.] "I love her deeply. I love her totally. Sir, I'd like your permission to take Mickey's hand in marriage!" [*"Imitating"* FATHER.] "Son, does my Mickey ever scare you?"

MICKEY: He never said that!

J.C.: [*"Playing"* SELF.] "Sir, she scares the crap out of me."

MICKEY: You never said that!

J.C.: [*"Imitating"* FATHER.] "Me too!" [*"Playing"* SELF.] "Sometimes I get the feeling she'd kill to get what she wants." [*"Imitating"* FATHER.] "Just like her Ma!"

MICKEY: I love it! I love it! More!! More!!!

J.C.: We laughed and laughed. He took my hand. God, what a grip! [*"Imitating"* FATHER.] "Son, what are your prospects?" [*"Playing"* SELF.] "I'm going to make a million by the time I'm 35."

MICKEY: Which you did! You did, indeed!!

J.C.: "When I get into my 50s, I'm going to have a big, long black limousine with a full-time driver named Jocko. Your daughter and I are going to drive up here from our duplex on Park Avenue. We're going to get out of our big long black limousine and your gorgeous daughter and I, we're going to sit on one of these benches just like you and I are right now, Mr. McGriff."

MICKEY: And what did my father say?

J.C.: [*"Imitating"* FATHER.] "Son, I do believe you'll do it!"

MICKEY: Father was right. We're here. Our limo's right over there. Jocko's driving. We do anything we want. Go anywhere we want. There's nothing we're without. We lack very little. We're kind, open, warm and generous. Our children call regularly. We all get together for Christmas. Tom never did finish Yale and Callie's had an awful time with all those different husbands but we couldn't be prouder. We're looked up to. Respected. People are always asking us out. God-o-God, if only Freddy Di Stephano, Archie Manning, and Cathy Nugent could see us now. [*Looks out over audience, sticks out tongue as though at old friends.*] Hey, you guys, look at who I ended up with!!! [*Puts arm around* J.C.] This man's a winner. This man's a champ. He's given me 26 years of sunshine and very few cloudy days. [*Waving to imaginary friends.*] Go ahead. Wave. Say "I'm J.C. I'm the great guy she ended up with!"

J.C.: There's no one there.

[MICKEY *takes* J.C.'S *hand and waves it for him. He pulls it away.*]

MICKEY: Boy, do I feel good. We're back. We're victorious. That's a big thing, to come back to Greenwich victorious. There's not much we've missed. We've missed very little.

J.C.: I miss getting here!

MICKEY: What?

J.C.: I look over at Jocko. [*Waving, yelling* O.S.] Hi, Jocko.

MICKEY: We won't be long, Jocko. [*Waving, yelling* O.S.] Isn't Greenwich lovely? Say hello to the swan. Go as close as you like.

J.C.: And seeing Jocko I realize the last thing I remember is getting into the car back on Park Avenue. I don't remember the turnpike. The turn-off at Exit 5. Was I good along the way? Was I kind and caring?

MICKEY: Darling, you hugged me all the way. At exits you kissed me and screamed. [*"Imitating"* J.C.] "We're here, my lovey's hometown!!!!"

J.C.: Any swear words?

MICKEY: None.

J.C.: No four-letters?

MICKEY: Not a one.

J.C.: Oh God, that's good. I worry so much. I've been praying every night. [*Suddenly gets to knees, folds hands prayerfully.*] "Dear Lord God, no four-letter words and make these days easy on my gal."

MICKEY: J.C., back here, please.

J.C.: What?

MICKEY: You're on your knees.

[*He looks down. Startled to find himself on the ground. Reaches out, tests ground to make sure it's true.*]

J.C.: How did I get here?

MICKEY: Stand up.

J.C.: [*Standing up.*] I'm standing.

MICKEY: Sit down.

J.C.: [*Sitting.*] I'm sitting. [*Pause.* J.C. *seems to go away and come back.*] I'll bet you were dandy.

MICKEY: What?

J.C.: Skating along. Flying by in your infamous outfit: white tights, short red skirt, red and white handwarmer, elf cap with—

MICKEY: We already did my skating.

[*Pause.*]

J.C.: When do we eat?

MICKEY: Soon.

J.C.: I'm famished.

MICKEY: Here. [*She takes her sandwich out of the wrapper and hands it to* J.C.]

J.C.: I heard you make those calls last week.

MICKEY: I didn't make any calls last week. Every time I go near the phone, you scream and yell and foam all over.

J.C.: His name was Davis. Fucking Frank Davis. You made plans to take me up there a week from next Thursday. Fucking Frank Davis'll put me in with someone from Jersey who can't stop drooling. There'll be drool all over me. I'll never stop wiping. They'll run out of towels... but you, you won't run out of towels. Your new guy's a towel salesman. You'll be on your honeymoon cruise and you'll be on your honeymoon deck on you way to Bermuda, and this Martin guy, your new guy, your Martin Podlofsky from Wayne, New Jersey, well, he'll bend over to give you his honeymoon special... only the howl of me will come screaming across the water and it'll surround you. My scream'll say [J.C. *lets out this scream low, sad and very intense. It is the cry of a desperate baby.*] No words. Just a plea from behind my padded walls. You'll try to pretend it's the wind, Martin'll say ["*Imitating*" MARTIN.] "Isn't that the moon?" But no, no, no, that's J.C. Webring and his scream will never let you kiss. Yessir, if you can eat without me, there's no—

[MICKEY *suddenly stuffs half a sandwich into* J.C.'s *mouth. He eats it down—seems about to resume diatribe but instead laughs gaily, and flaps hands like a little boy.*]

J.C.: [*Cont'd.*] I love when you feed me.

[*He bites off half of the second half and won't take anymore.* MICKEY *tries to feed last bite but he resists.*]

J.C.: [*Cont'd.*] If you feed me the last bite nice, I'll kiss you real sweet twice.

[*She feeds him his last bite. He kisses her, one kiss on each cheek.*]

J.C.: [*Cont'd.*] Wipe me clean. I've got crumbs in my beard.

[*She pretends to wipe crumbs out of "imaginary" beard.*]

J.C.: [*Cont'd.*] Brush it out nice. Make it look full.

[*She pretends to brush it off, fluffing out "imaginary" beard so it'll look full.* J.C. *smiles,* MICKEY, *too. For a second he seems fine. As if out of nowhere, he begins loudly singing a song.*]

J.C.: [*Cont.d*] When it comes early and you've still
got most of your hair
And your wife, she's dried up
She's run out of care
Who do you lean on?
Where do you run?
You're only 52
But your life's all done.

[MICKEY *covers* J.C.'S *mouth with hand. Holds it angrily.*]

MICKEY: You going to be good? [J.C. *shakes head "yes."*] Promise?!

[J.C. *again shakes head "yes."* MICKEY *lets go of his mouth.* J.C. *is suddenly hungry again.*]

J.C.: So, when do we eat?

MICKEY: J.C., we just did that!!!

[*Pause—long silence.* J.C. *suddenly raises hands like he's catching the warmth of the sun.*]

J.C.: Warm.

MICKEY: What?

J.C.: The sun.

MICKEY: Very.

J.C.: It's smiling down.

MICKEY: Indeed.

J.C.: Can I have some?

MICKEY: Some what?

J.C.: Sun on my wound. [*Pause.*] Doctor Mischler said the more ultra-violet I get on it, the quicker it would heal.

MICKEY: What a lovely breeze. Feel.

J.C.: I want it all sealed tight. I don't want any more loss. That's what I keep thinking.

MICKEY: What a lovely swan. Look. What a lovely day. Smile.

J.C.: That after they finished in there, they didn't stitch it tight enough and that's why lots of little pieces and loose ends keep slipping out.

[MICKEY *cannot take it anymore. She starts to scream, only covers her mouth. As* J.C. *talks on, it becomes harder and harder not to scream.*]

J.C.: [*Cont'd.*]That's where my memories are sliding. Out the little slits that aren't closing up fast enough. If someone real soon doesn't—

[*The pressure of holding blows her hand away. She removes hat.* J.C.'S *head is shaved. A huge scar is on left side of his head back to front, each of 100 stitches clearly visible.*]

J.C.: How's it look?

MICKEY: Good.

J.C.: No oozing?

MICKEY: None.

J.C.: The double stitches in the front?

MICKEY: Beautiful.

J.C.: By my ear?

MICKEY: All dried up.

J.C.: Toward the back.

MICKEY: I just told you, everything's—

J.C.: No, no. Itch toward the back. I want something new, smooth, and different! Do me smooth! Do me slow!!

[MICKEY *begins to rub his wound. She is smooth and slow.*]

J.C.: [*Cont'd.*] Left!

[MICKEY *moves left, continues smooth and slow.* J.C. *moans.*]

J.C.: [*Cont'd.*] Back!!

[MICKEY *moves to back. Rubs.* J.C. *now moans much more loudly.*]

J.C.: [*Cont'd.*] Now toward the front. Yes! Yes!! Circular, like you're buffing…Oh, God!! Do double strokes and then blow little puffs of air in my ear.

[MICKEY *does double strokes and blows little puffs in* J.C.'S *ear.
Moaning louder,* J.C. *suddenly grabs his groin—*MICKEY *slaps his
hand away.*]

J.C.: [*Cont'd.*] Sorry.

[MICKEY *continues to blow and rub.* J.C. *is having a horrible time
not grabbing his groin. He puts his hands every place but.*]

J.C.: [*Cont'd.*] Oh God! Oh God!! Rub and blow!! Rub and blow!!

[*Finally* J.C. *can't hold out. He grabs at his groin.* MICKEY *pulls
hand away, resumes rubbing. Again* J.C. *grabs groin, again* MICKEY
pulls hands away.]

MICKEY: If you're going to keep grabbing, I can't keep rubbing.

J.C.: It was your walk, you know. April 2, 1953. I was teeing off at
Innis Arden. I have a yellow tee. I set my #3 Titleist down. Take
a waggle, and see you walk. Your walk hooked me. Done there.
Stop rubbing and scratch, scratch all the way up front.

[MICKEY *does as* J.C. *asks. She stops rubbing, and scratches in front
of the wound.*]

J.C.: [*Cont'd.*] Harder, harder!!.

[*She rubs harder, he is aroused. Loud, screaming moan.*]

J.C.: [*Cont'd.*] I remember the first time I was in you. Boy, was I
warm and safe. The only other time I ever felt as warm and safe
was with a pitching wedge and I had 40 or 50 yards left to the
green.

MICKEY: We never did it before the honeymoon.

J.C.: Three times.

MICKEY: Not once.

J.C.: The first time was in the car by the eleventh green at Tamarack
up in back Greenwich!

MICKEY: I was pure. I earned my white organdie and silk.

J.C.: The second time—

MICKEY: Stop!

J.C.: Was after your dad took us out to dinner at Mamero's over on

Steamboat Road, and he fell asleep watching a TV movie. Great. Real fingernails. Deep—deep—deep.

MICKEY: Will you stop talking if I dig deep? I love when you're quiet. When you're quiet, I can stay with what I'm doing. When you're quiet, I can play you like an instrument. I hate talk. I don't mind mild moaning, but the constant patter, and the wild screams, well, they just make me want to vomit. I wish we could've . . . wish we—

J.C.: Why'd you stop?

[*She kisses* J.C.'S *head.*]

J.C.: [*Cont'd.*] You're always stopping. I was so close. I need you! I fucking goddamn need you. I can never do it by myself. I fucking require your rubs, your blows, and your fucking deep, deep scratches. [*Lets out scream.*] Look, the more I rub, the itchier it gets. I'm not a good rubber. I'm not a qualified scratcher.

[*Stops scratching, She looks away, not taking gloves.*]

J.C.: [*Cont'd.*] If you don't finish me, I'll read you my list.

MICKEY: There's no list.

J.C.: It's of all the women I've messed with when you weren't looking.

MICKEY: Don't lie. I'm your only!!

J.C.: March 22, 1962—Marge McClure in the parking lot outside the club during the Spring Solstice Dance. [MICKEY *covers ears.*] Please do me! Please finish me off!

[*He grabs* MICKEY'S *hands to free her ears to listen, but she puts them back. He tries again, she puts them back again.*]

J.C.: [*Cont'd.*] April 3, 13, 21, 28 plus . . . May 8, 9 and 10, 1966. You were in the hospital for a D-and-C, right, well, I did it all those times with this waitress from up at Adams Corner.

MICKEY: No, no, no, I'm your only!!!

J.C.: October 7, 1971 with . . . and then November 1974 . . . no, 1975 with . . . and, of course, for-three straight summers, 81 through 83 with . . . Always cutting me off. Always leaving me short. Never there when I ache!! Always turning away when I bleed!!

[*He punches at his groin over and over like it was the most unreliable friend a man could possibly have.*]

Fuck! Piss! Shit! Bleed! Ache! Die!!
Fuck! Piss! Shit! Bleed! Ache! Die!!
Fuck! Piss! Shit! Bleed! Ache! Die!!

[*He stops. He goes through still another change. As dark as he was, he now is light and bright and full of smiles. He takes her hands away from her ears. Suddenly he grabs at the top of his head as though some minor miracle had transpired.*] The itching's gone and you did it. [*Picks up hat and puts it on. Poses proudly.*] I look normal. I look nice. I can pass another rich guy keeping it simple!

[MICKEY *tries to smile but she begins to cry. She sobs.* J.C. *smiles broadly.*]

J.C.: [*Cont'd.*] Finally I'm needed.

MICKEY: Are you?

J.C.: You're crying.

MICKEY: [*Touching eyes.*] Am I?

J.C.: Can I kiss them off?

MICKEY: Gently. One at a time.

[J.C. *reaches and begins kissing tears off* MICKEY'S *face. She's ecstatic. Suddenly* J.C. *does a slurping sound and licks, swallows and wipes away a wide bunch at once.*]

MICKEY: [*Cont'd.*] I wish you'd been gentler. I wish you'd studied the Europeans. They never rush. Never skip steps. Never get ahead!

[*Now* MICKEY *bursts into a river of tears. Sobs that come from a deep place. She suddenly stops sobbing and pushes* J.C. *away.*]

MICKEY: [*Cont'd.*] I'm crying. I need care. I need lips. What happened to your lips? Where's your care?!

J.C.: Look!

[J.C. *points off in direction behind bench.* MICKEY *looks around, finally sees where* J.C.'S *pointing.*]

MICKEY: Why's Jocko waving? Why does he keep pointing to his wrist?

J.C.: Eddy Joe Tammany's due any minute.

MICKEY: Tom's boyhood friend. The short little thing with a cowlick who always passed Tom the ball. Hold it! Why's he—

J.C.: He's doing the driving.

MICKEY: Where to?

J.C.: Here's your ticket.

[*From breast pocket* J.C. *removes AA plane ticket. He hands it to* MICKEY.]

MICKEY: Champagne First Class to San Francisco! God, we haven't been to Frisco—

J.C.: San Francisco!!

MICKEY: San Francisco since...since Tom was 17. He'd led the Southern Connecticut Catholic league in scoring and rebounding both.

J.C.: He was taller than everyone. What happened at Yale?

MICKEY: And Callie, she was just starting— [*Suddenly stops.*] Hold it! Where's your ticket?

[J.C. *pulls road map of U.S. out of pocket and spreads it out on bench. He is like a little kid.*]

J.C.: Red is our route. Blue are the places we stay over. Every night. I'll be calling you from a blue. Look—Wheeling, West Virginia—Springfield, Illinois—Lander, Wyoming. See, 13 days, 13 stops, 13 calls. "It's Wyoming, Mickey, but boy do I miss you!"

MICKEY: What about the three big green circles?

J.C.: Those are the two-day layovers to play golf. Oakmont, Pittsburgh. Cherry Hills, Denver and last but not least, Pebble Beach. Thirteen days from now I'll be at Pebble Beach. I'll be standing on the sixth tee at Pebble looking down the fairway of this incredible 5-par that's surrounded by cliffs and ocean and back here you'll be at JFK boarding American flight #1 to come join me. I smash my drive, your 747 rockets into the air. We're both airborne. We're both looking forward to a reunion. A reunion? Why? 'Cause we've had the courage to take a break. A pause—a res...res...

MICKEY: Respite!

J.C.: You've always known more words. See, lately, we've been really—no, not we! Me!! I've been worse than ever—oh, God!

MICKEY: What?

J.C.: The sun's back on. [*Takes off hat. Again the "incredible scar."*] In the morning when I first look at you...well...I just want...I mean, you look tired. Awful. Defeated. Beaten. I lock myself in the bathroom with my golf books, go practice my putting in my attic, take a walk down by the water. It doesn't matter what, and I cry. Cry, I mean it. I slump over and real tears flow. Why? I've made you old. I've robbed your beauty. But, Mickey, 13 days and you'll get a lot of it back. Now, I know how scary it is for you to—

MICKEY: What hotel?

J.C.: Come again?

MICKEY: In San Francisco.

J.C.: You mean you'll—

MICKEY: Which hotel, J.C., is it the Mark Hopkins?

J.C.: Jocko made the reservations. Check with him on the way home.

[MICKEY *gets up and starts to walk off. She is smiling hugely.*]

MICKEY: Good luck!

J.C.: Aren't you even going to—

MICKEY: See you in 13 days!

J.C.: But don't you want to—

[MICKEY *exits toward* JOCKO *and the waiting limousine.* J.C. *looks around nervously. Gets to feet—waves like a nervous diver about to attempt his last dive.*]

J.C.: [*Cont'd.*] Good-bye, Greenwich! Good luck, Connecticut!! [J.C. *starts toward pond a.k.a. the audience. Suddenly he is aware that his head is uncovered. He goes back to bench and puts on hat. He stands there several seconds. Addresses world around him.*] Good-bye, trees, bushes and birds and all other valued and living things.

[*He suddenly charges toward pond. Out of nowhere* MICKEY *comes on and tackles* J.C. *to the ground. He struggles to get away but* MICKEY *will not let go.* J.C. *screams and yells,* MICKEY *laughs.*]

MICKEY: You almost had me fooled. The hotel reservations gave you away.

J.C.: Let me go.

MICKEY: No, no, no.

J.C.: Let me jump in. Let me go under. Let me dive in and go directly to the bottom. I want to lie on my back. Count the ducks, open my mouth, and let the water all in. I want to—want to . . . [*Pause.*] I can't anymore—I can't—I can't.

MICKEY: Can't what!!

J.C.: I can't get in the car on Park Avenue, and wake up here. I can't come to anymore, and see your eyes all scared and hurt. I can't—

[*He once more tries to break away and jump into the pond, but* MICKEY *holds him back.*]

J.C.: [*Cont'd.*] Every morning when I wake up, I tell myself, "J.C., don't go away today. Stay here, stay in the now!" But somehow, I keep slipping away, and . . . and the harder I try not to, the more it comes.

MICKEY: J.C.?

J.C.: When I go away, am I still me? Do I talk the same? Do I kiss different? I can't stand the not-knowing!

MICKEY: Your not-knowing's all over!

[*She hands him present-wrapped package. He slowly opens it. It is a small cassette recorder. For a second he's baffled, but then he gets it. He claps his hands like a little boy.*]

J.C.: Every time I go away?

MICKEY: I'll press RECORD.

J.C.: And then when I come back?

MICKEY: I'll press STOP!

J.C.: Then you'll press REWIND.

MICKEY: And together we'll listen to where you've been. It'll all be different for me, hearing it not alone. I can't stand it alone. I hate things by myself.

J.C.: Why didn't I think of it first?

MICKEY: When things get bad, I see clear.

[*They laugh together.*]

J.C.: And, you're always ahead of me. You pretend like you're behind but, Mickey, thank God for the things you think of. Wow, the places you go—wow, I'm glad you're here! [*Suddenly* J.C. *freezes. A whole new mood comes over him.*] Please press RECORD

[MICKEY *presses PLAY.* J.C. *looks around as if he just woke up. Takes* MICKEY'S *hand. She smiles. He smiles confusedly.*]

MICKEY: Are you O.K.?

J.C.: Who are you?

[*SLOW FADE*]

END OF PLAY

William Seebring

THE ORIGINAL LAST WISH BABY

WILLIAM SEEBRING

William Seebring grew up in rural Ohio. After leaving home for a well-paying factory job which did not suit him, Seebring drove a 1965 Pontiac LeSabre to Brooklyn where he taught himself the basics of structural and anatomical drawing. Adopting the pseudonym, Douglas Michael, Seebring published a series of underground comic books as well as an illustrated full-color travel guide to fictitious lands that were published, strangely enough, by a magazine catering to singles.

In 1986, Seebring returned to Ohio and bought a Honda Accord. Four years later, he moved to upstate New York with his wife and their dog where he began adapting his comix to stage plays while maintaining one of the finest cars ever assembled in North America. Under his assumed name, Seebring has dabbled in too many pursuits to mention including literary agent and country and western songwriter.

His only other completed plays to date are *The Gelding*s, a western spoof about cowboys who have no genitals and *Das Wolfkin*, a darkly comic fairy tale written in an invented language.

CHARACTERS

There are as many as forty characters including thirty-seven speaking parts; however, the play can be performed with as few as five actors. A suggested breakdown of parts are divided as follows:

NARRATOR   male or female

ACTOR #1   male: Executive, Specialist #1, Customer #1, Crown-Features-Marketeer, Newsboy, Phoney-Last-Wish-Baby, Diner, Right-To-Extended-Lifer #2

ACTOR #2   female: Spokesmodel, Specialist #3, Welda Mae Forms, Network-Exec #3, Waitress, Guatemalan woman, Maitre d', Pundit #3, Right-To-Extended-Lifer #1, Pollster

ACTOR #3   male: Doctor, Man, Specialist #2, Network-Exec #2, Customer #2, Crown-Features-Pitchman, Lawyer, Daryl Wayne Trebleau, Pundit #2, Surgeon, Preacher, Politician #2

ACTOR #4   female: Nurse, Assistant, Ms. Kornfeld, Network Exec #1, Clara Collins, Crown-Features-Exec, Judge, Pundit #1, Politician #1

SETS: *Aside from a podium, the action of the play is best staged with pools of lighting and minor propping.*

Before rise, we hear tha-dump, tha-dump—the steady, rhythmic beat of a human heart. As this beat grows in base and intensity, a slide is projected. The slide s of a graphic of THE LAST WISH BABY. *As the beat slowly fades,* LIGHTS *come up on the narrator standing at a podium at far stage-right.*

NARRATOR: *The Original Last Wish Baby*, as researched, recorded and revised by William Seebring.

[*A* SLIDE *graphic of Cleveland, Ohio.*]

Cleveland, Ohio. Or, more specifically, the third-floor maternity room of the Holy Name Hospital on Cleveland's impoverished west-side where, at precisely seven-oh-one P.M.—

[SLIDE *graphic of an inner city hospital. We hear a crying baby.*]

A baby was born. Not just any baby, but the infamous, original, Last Wish Baby. The baby born without a heart.

[*Lights up on a* DOCTOR *and* NURSE *peering in on an infant's crib.*]

DOCTOR: No heart? Good Heavens, that's impossible.

NURSE: Check for yourself, Doctor.

[*The* DOCTOR *extends his stethoscope into the crib.*]

DOCTOR: Nothing, no pulse. Not a sound. And yet, this baby clearly mimics life. A freak.

NURSE: [*Softly.*] No. A miracle.

DOCTOR: What's that?

NURSE: A miracle... the baby is a miracle.

DOCTOR: A miracle? This is Cleveland. It'll be a miracle if the mother's insured.

[*Lights down on the maternity ward.*]

NARRATOR: Not only were the baby's parents uninsured, the identity of the baby's father was unknown. However, the birth mother's name was given as Welda Mae Forms, a thirty-one-year-old unemployed cosmetologist.

[SLIDE *graphic of* WELDA MAE FORMS.]

At the time, little else was known about Ms. Forms but word of her remarkable progeny spread quickly from the maternity ward to the scrub rooms to the hospital's administrative offices where a larger picture began to emerge.

[*Lights up on the Hospital's Administrative* EXECUTIVE *and his* ASSISTANT.]

EXECUTIVE: A baby born without a heart? Sounds awful. Sounds really awful.

ASSISTANT: Maybe not as bad as you think.

EXECUTIVE: C'mon Chet, how the hell do ya' window dress a missing heart? God knows we've had our share of high-risk deliveries here at Holy Name—little baby heads get smushed, tiny baby limbs get... it's messy, terrible, makes me shudder. But delivering a baby and not the heart—good God! [*Beat.*] What's our liability on something like that?

ASSISTANT: Well here's the thing, sir . . . the baby is alive.

EXECUTIVE: Alive? Without a heart? But that's, that's—

ASSISTANT: Impossible? Yes. Nevertheless, it's true.

EXECUTIVE: What—some kind of weird, auto-neuron tremors? Good God, is that what passes for life these days?

ASSISTANT: The baby is fully functioning, quite spirited and has a healthy appetite I might add.

EXECUTIVE: But for how long? An hour, maybe two?

ASSISTANT: Who can say? But, even if the baby were to, God forbid . . . Its short life could, with the right spin, be played out as the most incredible P.R. story of our time. What's more, the timing couldn't have been more . . . fortuitous . . . sir.

EXECUTIVE: What, the Sprag/Klockenheim takeover?

ASSISTANT: Precisely the kind of thing that could triple our name factor overnight. A miracle . . . and it happened here, in our hospital, under the care and guidance of our health care professionals. Think of it sir, *Holy Name, the get-well place where miracles happen.*

EXECUTIVE: *The get-well place where miracles happen* . . . Now there's a ball with some bounce to it! Call Delores Childs at Channel Five. If we can dazzle her, there's a good chance we could make the six o'clock news!

ASSISTANT: She's on her way, sir.

EXECUTIVE: Good boy. Oh, one other thing . . . the heart? Did anyone ever find the heart?

ASSISTANT: No. Actually, as far anyone knows, there never was a heart.

[*Lights down on the administrative offices.*]

NARRATOR: In point of fact, there was a heart. However, through one of those unfathomable anomalies which defy all logic, yet govern most things, the heart was delivered separately by a surprised New Jersey woman on her way home from the store.

[*Lights up on* MS. SYDNEY KORNFELD, *as she crosses the stage car-*

rying a Nordstrom's bag. She is walking past a MAN *when something like a beef-steak tomato falls from her skirt. The man regards it.* MS. KORNFELD *continues on, unmindful.*]

MAN: Yo, Miss . . . Ma'am! You dropped something.

[MS. KORNFELD *stops, turns and looks back.*]

MS. KORNFELD: Oh-my-god, what is it!

[*The sound of a thumping heart is heard as lights dim on* MS. KORNFELD *as she bends to retrieve the heart.*]

NARRATOR: That something would later be determined to be the baby's heart. However, at that particular moment, the New Jersey woman, later identified as Ms. Sydney Kornfeld, and who would soon become known as "The Baby Heart Mom," was not yet aware of the miracle baby story unfolding in Cleveland.

[SLIDE *of a graphic reading:* THE FOLLOWING IS SPONSORED BY LIBBY'S AND THE TUPPERWARE CORPORATION. *Lights up as a* DEMONSTRATOR *enters carrying a tupperware container, a beef-steak tomato, and a can of peaches.*]

NARRATOR: As for Ms. Kornfeld, she fortuitously retrieved the baby heart and returned immediately to her home in Paramus where, as the demonstrator shall faithfully recreate, she placed the pulsating vital organ into a clear, air-tight, number-seven tupperware container, which she then filled with a high-fructose, low sodium, heavy-syrup drained from a can of Libby's yellow-cling sliced peaches. After burping for a tight seal, Ms. Kornfeld placed the container in the crisper drawer of her refrigerator where, according to product designers, the heart could have been stored indefinitely and would remain every bit as fresh and vigorous as the moment she delivered it.

[*Lights down as the* DEMONSTRATOR *exits.*]

NARRATOR: [*Cont'd.*] Meanwhile, back in Cleveland, Ohio, ever more adept medical specialists were brought in to examine the so-called miracle baby.

[*Lights up on the maternity ward as three medical* SPECIALISTS *look into a crib and we hear a giggling baby.*]

SPECIALIST #1: Coo-chee-coo-chee-cooo.

SPECIALIST #2: No pulse. No pressure. This baby doesn't have a heart.

SPECIALIST #3: I'll be damned.

SPECIALIST #2: And yet...this baby is alive.

[*The Hospital's Executive* ASSISTANT *enters. He appears agitated.*]

ASSISTANT: Doctors, please, the press conference. They're waiting.

[*Lights down on the maternity ward. Lights up as the* THREE SPE-CIALISTS *and the* ASSISTANT *take their places at a table facing the audience. The table skirt advertises the Holy Name Hospital and its new slogan. The* NARRATOR *assumes the role of reporter.*]

ASSISTANT: [*Cont'd.*] Questions for the doctors?

NARRATOR: Yes. A living baby without a heart? How is this possible?

SPECIALIST #2: Technically, it's not.

SPECIALIST #1: The baby should be dead.

SPECIALIST #3: In fact, the baby could die any minute.

ASSISTANT: It's a miracle is what it is! And it happened right here in our—

NARRATOR: What about the baby's mom?

ASSISTANT: What about her?

NARRATOR: I'd like to hear her side of the story. I'd like to ask her a few questions.

ASSISTANT: [*Horrified.*] What, you mean talk with her?

NARRATOR: Why not?

ASSISTANT: No reason, uh, well, actually—that's impossible. I'm sorry, we're just, she's just—she's in recovery right now.

[*Lights down on the Press Conference.*]

NARRATOR: In fact, Welda Mae Forms was not in recovery. The so-called Baby Mom was not only alert and well-rested, she was, much to the dismay of hospital staffers, quite lucid and most out-spoken.

[*Lights up on* WELDA MAE FORMS, *in bed and under restraint. The* EXECUTIVE *and his* ASSISTANT *hover.*]

WELDA MAE FORMS: What's with the god-damned seat belts! And where's my kid! I come into this dump to pop off another slug, which is the last thing I need, and you-all got me tied down so I can't even see Oprah—big as she is!

EXECUTIVE: Ms. Forms, please, please calm down. There's something we have to tell you.

WELDA MAE FORMS: What, is my baby dead, or deformed, or some damn thing?

ASSISTANT: Uh, well, Miss Forms, actually, it's more than that.

WELDA MAE FORMS: Huh? Was that a hard question or are you really as stupid as you look? Listen here lap-dog, tell your fat ass boss that as far as I'm concerned I could care less if the little maggot's dead or mutated—hell, I never wanted one tuh begin with. Tried to have it flushed out in one of them clinics but them damn bible-thumpers chased me away and—

EXECUTIVE: [*Aghast.*] You were going to...! Cleveland's miracle baby...?

WELDA MAE FORMS: So, I figured I'd drown the slug in booze. Well, did it work or what?

EXECUTIVE: Ms. Forms, you've got to understand... you've made medical history here today.

WELDA MAE FORMS: Hee-doggie! Do tell, the little maggot's got three heads? Two weenies? Five titties? What? What?!

ASSISTANT: This is insane. We can't put that before the public. She'll ruin everything!

[*Lights down on* WELDA MAE's *hospital room.*]

NARRATOR: Meanwhile, at that very moment, the afternoon press conference was being fed via satellite to network studios in New York.

[*Lights up on a roomful of* NETWORK EXECS *watching a monitor.*]

NETWORK EXEC #1: Can this be for real, a baby without a heart?!

NETWORK EXEC #2: The affiliate swears it's true.

NETWORK EXEC #3: Regardless, it's too late to break tonight.

NETWORK EXEC #1: Are you nuts! This stuff goes on immediately.

NETWORK EXEC #3: But, but we're airing a live feed from the White House!

NETWORK EXEC #2: Who cares? A baby without a heart! Now that's news!

[LIGHTS *down on the* NETWORK EXECS.]

NARRATOR: And news it was. Within the hour, satellite-beaming reporters from around the world had descended on Cleveland like the plague and every last one of them wanted one thing—a baby mom exclusive. Hospital officials acted with both haste and prudence.

[*Lights up on* WELDA MAE'S *hospital room.* WELDA *is still under restraint.* CLARA COLLINS, *a stylishly dressed woman, enters.*]

WELDA MAE FORMS: Who are you? What do ya' want?

CLARA COLLINS: Hello, Ms. Forms. My name is Clara Collins, I've been hired to be your image consultant.

WELDA MAE FORMS: Oh yeah? Well, does that mean you can reach up there and change the channel on the god-damned TV? Because that's all I've been trying to get from the lazy turds in white that run around here all day. And do they listen? Hell, no. Channel five—wrestling. You get me Bone-Crusher on the tube and a lay a six-pack of Huedey Gold right here 'side my pillow and I'll be so happy I could pee green.

CLARA COLLINS: Well, I see I have my work cut out for me.

[*Lights down on* WELDA's *room.*]

NARRATOR: Clara Collins proved she was worth every penny of her hefty fee. In short order, Ms. Welda Mae Forms was polished, enlightened and coiffured. At long last, cameras were admitted into her room and a nation known for its thirst of spectacle, tuned in.

[*Lights up on* WELDA's *room. She is no longer restrained and her appearance has been transformed. Religious music is piped in and a* SLIDE *is projected of babies with angel wings and angel halos.*]

WELDA MAE FORMS: [*Her hands folded as if in prayer.*] With the Lord's help, my precious, precious baby will live. Of course, I can't begin to thank all you wonderful little people out there who have kept me and my baby in your thoughts and prayers. Bless you. Bless you all.

[*Lights down on* WELDA'S *room.*]

NARRATOR: With that one newsbit, the groundswell of public emotion became unquenchable. Overnight, Cleveland's miracle tot became America's most adored critical-list baby. There were news conferences every morning and afternoon and updates on the baby's condition flashed every hour on the hour, but it wasn't enough. Americans not only wanted to know more, they wanted to know what more they could do . . .

[*Lights up on a lunch-counter somewhere deep in rural America.*]

WAITRESS: And they say that baby could die any moment.

CUSTOMER #1: Hate to see that baby die and me not knowing if they was something I coulda' done.

CUSTOMER #2: By Gawd, I'd give my left nut for that sweet, little innocent lamb.

WAITRESS: Hell, Ross, baby don't need a go-nad. That baby needs a heart!

CUSTOMER #2: Can't give baby my heart. But I'd give that baby anything else. Anything a'tall.

CUSTOMER #1: Say, you know I hear baby likes to watch big time wrestling! What say we call the hospital and see if we could buy that baby a brand new color TV! Now wouldn't that make us all feel a whole sight better?

[*Lights down on the lunch counter.*]

NARRATOR: Calls from like-minded Americans jammed the hospital's switch-board. It was reported that in a single, twenty-four hour period more than twenty thousand color TV's were bought and delivered. Corporate America stood up and took note. Syndicate giant, GLAM ENTERTAINMENT, culled their best minds and put forward a most alluring concept.

[SLIDE *Graphic of Glam Entertainment logo. Lights up on an executive board meeting.*]

GLAM ENTERTAINMENT PITCHMAN: Every night we'll feature the baby mom, what's her name—

GLAM ENTERTAINMENT MARKETEER: Welda Mae Forms.

GLAM ENTERTAINMENT EXEC: Welda Mae? Where do you gotta' go to get a name like that?

GLAM ENTERTAINMENT MARKETEER: Welda, last stop before Zelda.

GLAM ENTERTAINMENT PITCHMAN: Whatever, we get her and we call it, "The Last Wish Baby Show." See, every night mom stands in front of the camera holding little baby no-heart in her arms like this and she's pouting 'cause the doc's are telling her how the baby's supposed to die any minute but, and here's the kicker, before baby goes, baby's made this one last wish . . . get it? Baby's last wish—Last Wish Baby!

[Eyes widen with delight. Lights down on the meeting.]

NARRATOR: A deal was proffered and quickly struck with Ms. Forms and her people. That very night, "The Last Wish Baby Show" blew out the ratings board with a whopping 75 share. Even more notable, the show's seamless tie-in with corporate sponsors set an industry standard.

[SLIDE graphic of "The Last Wish Baby Show." Lights up on WELDA's *hospital room. A TV camera crew crowd* WELDA *as she clutches a cloth-wrapped bundle in her arms.]*

WELDA MAE FORMS: Poor, poor baby. Baby doesn't have a heart. Doctors say baby might have to leave us all for Heaven any minute now.

[We hear the baby cry.]

WELDA MAE FORMS: *[Cont'd.]* What's that Baby . . . ? *[After leaning in to the baby,* WELDA *returns her gaze to the cameras.]* Awww. Baby wishes some nice person out there would buy us a uh . . . a Sony XRK-35 Digital Game System.

NARRATOR: *[In an announcer's voice.]* That's right folks, the Sony game system could be Baby's Last Wish. Poor Baby. So open up that heart God so kindly gave you and call the 1-800 number you see now on your screen.

[SLIDE of the 1-800 number. Lights down on The Last Wish Baby

Show. Lights up on MS. KORNFELD'*s kitchen where a* GUATEMALAN CLEANING WOMAN *removes a tupperware container and pops it open.*]

NARRATOR: [*Cont'd.*] Meanwhile, in a certain kitchen in Paramus, New Jersey, a certain Guatemalan cleaning woman was wiping down a certain refrigerator when she made an unusual discovery.

GUATEMALAN WOMAN: Eeeeee! Mios Dios! Eeeee!

[MS. KORNFELD *enters.*]

MS. KORNFELD: What? Que? Que esta? What the hell is it?

GUATEMALAN WOMAN: Esta la corazón de la nino con last wish!

MS. KORNFELD: What? What are you talking about?

GUATEMALAN WOMAN: Nino! Nino con last wish! Nino con last wish!

MS. KORNFELD: Baby? You mean that baby? That Last Wish baby? The one on TV? Give me that! [*Studies the heart for a moment.*] Oh-my-God, it's alive! I have the baby heart! What should I do? What should I do?

GUATEMALAN WOMAN: Llama de medico! Pronto! Pronto!

MS. KORNFELD: Call a doctor?! Are you crazy? This is big, really big! I'm calling Howard Stern!

[MS. KORNFELD *reaches for the phone. Lights down.*]

NARRATOR: Ms. Kornfeld's call to the popular radio shock jock was quickly put through and she not only revealed that she possessed what she believed was the Last Wish Baby's Heart, listeners also learned her cup size and that she enjoyed lesbian sex while a sophomore at Harley Dickerson University.

[SLIDE *graphic of a woman's bra.* SLIDE *graphic of two campus coeds.*]

Meanwhile, word of the whereabouts of the newly discovered baby heart spread fast and a race, of sorts, was on. EMS crews were first on the scene but no sooner had they readied the baby heart for shipment to Cleveland when... the lawyers arrived.

[*Lights up on a* LAWYER *waving a writ.*]

LAWYER: Halt! Court order!

[*Lights down on the* LAWYER.]

NARRATOR: Motions were made. Injunctions issued. Larger questions loomed. The battle for custody of the Last Wish Baby had begun.

[*We hear the thumping heart.* SLIDE *graphic of the baby heart.*]

The hearing to determine the rightful custodial parents of The Last Wish Baby had barely opened when legal fees threatened to exceed even Ms. Welda Mae Forms' recently fatted purse-strings. However, with the baby show still posting record ratings, Ms. Forms saw fit to make full use of her forum.

[*Lights up on "The Last Wish Baby Show" set.* SLIDE *graphic of the show's logo.*]

WELDA MAE FORMS: [*Angelic.*] Poor, poor precious baby. Baby doesn't have a heart...know why? Hmmm? [*Bitter.*] 'Cause some East Coast floozy has got it and won't hand it over unless I give her half a' baby's royalties on the—

[*The baby cries.* WELDA *looks down.*]

WELDA MAE FORMS: [*Cont'd.*] Yeah, what is it? [*A beat to compose herself.*] Awww, but of course, baby. [WELDA *looks up again and composes herself.*] Baby wishes there was some nice, pro-bono law firm out there who would take Baby's rightful mother's custody case, and when that was all settled, and a certain individual from a certain so-called Garden-State was financially ruined, that same nice law firm might just be retained to negotiate with those shysters at Glum Entertainment for a more favorable contract...idn't that what baby wants? Yes, baby's so sweet. I just hope and pray this won't be baby's last wish.

[WELDA *smiles sweetly as lights darken on "The Last Wish Baby Show."*]

NARRATOR: But, no sooner had Welda Mae and her people retained new legal counsel than a shocking courtroom revelation hit the newsstands.

[*Lights up on a* NEWSBOY *hawking his papers.*]

NEWSBOY: Read all about it! "Last Wish Baby Show" Hoax! Read all about it!

[*Lights down on the* NEWSBOY.]

NARRATOR: Unsealed court documents alleged that the "Last Wish

Baby Show" Baby was not the real Last Wish Baby, the baby born without a heart, but rather, a sixteen-year-old unemployed actor with a glandular condition. Americans shuddered. Did this mean the Original Last Wish Baby was dead? Or, Heaven forbid, was there even an original Last Wish Baby in the first place? Congressional spouses convened a hearing and demanded answers.

[SLIDE *graphic of congressional spouses. Lights up on a hearing room.* WELDA MAE, *the Hospital's Executive* ASSISTANT *and the* PHONY LAST WISH BABY *are seated together under a glaring light. The* NARRATOR *serves as inquisitor.*]

NARRATOR: [*Cont'd.*] Come forward. State your full name and occupation for the record, please.

PHONY LAST WISH BABY: Look pal, you can't nail this one on me! I'm not even Equity! The only reason I signed on to this sham was 'cause the Lady there got me tanked-up, then threatened to put my nuts in the grinder if I didn't—

WELDA MAE FORMS: Shut your trap you little—

PHONY LAST WISH BABY: Who are you calling little!? The only thing little around here is your heart! You wanna' know why her kid's got no heart? I'll tell ya' why—

WELDA MAE FORMS: How dare you! And you said you loved me!

ASSISTANT: Stop it! Okay, look, it was all my fault. I agreed to pull the baby from the show and I was the one who okayed it when the Forms woman wanted to hire the little guy. But I only went along with it 'cause the doctors insisted on keeping the baby in intensive care. That's the God's-honest truth. There really is a Last Wish Baby, there really is a baby without a heart! I can prove it! I swear to God, I can prove it!

[*Lights down on the hearing room.*]

NARRATOR: Needless to say, Americans were skeptical and demanded that proof. Thus, the following night, "The Last Wish Baby Show" aired live from the Holy Name Hospital's pediatric intensive care unit. Viewers held their breath as the Baby Mom ushered the cameras toward the swinging doors which led to Baby's chamber.

[SLIDE *graphic of the "Last Wish Baby Show." Lights up on a hospital corridor.* WELDA MAE *and the* ASSISTANT *are wearing scrubs.* WELDA MAE *motions for the cameraman to follow her through a pair of doors.*]

WELDA MAE FORMS: Shhhh. Be quiet. This way, please.

[*A man* DARYL WAYNE TREBLEU *pushes by the* ASSISTANT *toward* WELDA.]

ASSISTANT: Watch it, he's got a gun!

[*Suddenly, the stage goes black. Four gunshots are heard and we see a series of quick* SLIDES *projecting images of chaos. The screen fills with the Emergency Broadcast test image and an accompanying high-pitched hum. This hum fades and the lights come up on the* NARRATOR.]

NARRATOR: Four shots, each one following its own fatal trajectory, were fired into the torso and cranial cavity of the woman most Americans knew only as the Last Wish Baby Mom.

[SLIDE *graphic of a "mug-shot" of* DARYL WAYNE TREBLEU.]

The assailant was identified as Daryl Wayne Trebleu, a slope-shouldered, itinerant floral designer from nearby Loraine, Ohio, and, purportedly, the man many believed to be the Last Wish Baby Dad.

[*Lights up on* DARYL WAYNE TREBLEU *standing solemnly.*]

Daryl Wayne Trebleu never uttered a single word in his own defense. Rather, he expressed himself through artfully-designed floral arrangements.

[SLIDE *graphic of* DARYL'S *bouquet.*]

Mr. Trebleu's "Not competent to stand trial bouquet" was a lovely and eloquent display of mums, gladiolus, and forty-four magnum shell casings set in a handsome earthenware bowl. Meanwhile, in another court in another state, the judge in the custody hearing for the Last Wish Baby had reached a verdict.

[*Lights down on* DARYL WAYNE TREBLEU. *Lights up on a* JUDGE *behind his bench.*]

JUDGE: As per the dictates of the honorable State of New Jersey, court of Domestic Relations, I, Judge Maliss T. Ward Nunn, have found as follows: Said infant, here-in-and-ever-after known as, "The Original Last Wish Baby," shall be granted ward status of this court, and thereby ordered to be joined immediately with heart. So be it, so help us God.

[*The* JUDGE *pounds his gavel. Lights fade on his courtroom.* SLIDE *graphics of close-in shots of medical procedures.*]

NARRATOR: With the Last Wish Baby Show having been abruptly pulled from the airwaves, no effort was made to appeal the Judge's decision. Thus, a medical team of the nation's leading cardio-vascular surgeons were assembled to carry out the court's wishes and, with God's blessing, prolong the baby's life. Meanwhile, high-minded pontificators from the academic, medical and legal communities pondered the implications of it all for the benefit of viewers at home.

[*Lights up on a televised round-table show.*]

PUNDIT #1: The baby phenomenon speaks directly to who we are as a nation.

PUNDIT #2: And who we, as a nation, are not.

PUNDIT #3: Yes, who we are, and who we are not.

PUNDIT #1: But more to who we are than who we are not.

PUNDIT #3: Then again, I think one could say this whole baby phenomena says even more still to where we, as a nation, are going than where we, as a nation, have been.

PUNDIT #2: Or not been.

PUNDIT #1: Or not, not been.

PUNDIT #2: Or not been, not been not.

PUNDIT #3: Yes, not been not. But not, been-been, not-not, been-not-been.

[*This absurd chorus continues for a beat or two until:*]

NARRATOR: We interrupt this program to bring you a special Last Wish Baby medical update. We take you now live, directly to the Hoppscotch Medical Center in Tarmack, New Jersey.

[*Lights down on the pundits. Lights up on a bloody* SURGEON.]

SURGEON: The operation to implant the baby heart into the Last Wish Baby was both...a success and...a failure. The heart was successfully sutured and continues to pump vigorously. Unfortunately, the baby, for reasons we do not fully understand, has ceased all other life sustaining functions and...appears to be in a rapid state of...decay.

[*Lights down on the surgeon. A series of* SLIDE *graphics showing the Last Wish Baby in varying states of decay. All the while we hear the thumping of the baby heart.*]

NARRATOR: There was no denying it. The Original Last Wish Baby, the baby born without a heart, was now, and irretrievably, a dead baby, but one with a very healthy heart. And that presented doctors and lawyers with an entirely new set of problems. For one, the baby could not be considered legally dead unless the heart were either stopped or removed. However, if the baby was not legally dead, then removing or stopping the heart would be, in a word, murder. Therefore, despite all appearances to the contrary, the Last Wish Baby was, in the eyes of the law, very much alive. Further, this being a democratic society, it didn't take long for Americans to gaze upon their own dearly departed loved ones and find similar cause to stretch the definition of what constitutes life...and death.

[*The thumping fades. Lights up in a restaurant where a* MAITRE D' *is calling out.*]

MAITRE D': Chatterwok, party of four, your table is ready. Chatterwok, party of four—

[*Suddenly, a* DINER *wheels in a corpse dressed in evening wear. The* MAITRE D' *is appalled.*]

MAITRE D': Excusé-moi, monsieur! Excusé—Yo! What in God's name do you think you're doing?

DINER: Look here buddy...my wife may look a little ripe to you, but she's still getting mail, and that, in my opinion, qualifies her for your early bird special. Oh, and uh, non-smoking section, please.

[*Lights down on the restaurant.*]

NARRATOR: Suddenly, Americans became embroiled in an entirely new moral debate—when did life end? The question was not at all as simple as it sounded. After all, who in this country can say with any real certainty when life begins?

[*Lights up on a* PREACHER'S *pulpit.*]

PREACHER: As the Bible so specifically tells us and I say unto you, brethren, Dust to dust!

ALL: Dust to dust.

[*Lights down on the* PREACHER.]

NARRATOR: With those words, the "Right to Extended Life" movement was born. Also known as "Anti-Funeralists," the movement cannily usurped the image of The Last Wish Baby and made it their own. Soon, that image was being bandied about as a symbol of protest in nearly every cemetery and crematorium in the country.

[*Lights up on a funeral as* MOURNERS *stand over an open grave.*]

MOURNER: Bill was...he was a decent guy. A sensible guy. The kind of guy who let you know where he stood even when everything else around just got weirder and weirder—

[*Two* RIGHT TO EXTENDED LIFERS *enter and march around. They are wearing Last Wish Baby/Anti-Funeralists t-shirts.*]

RIGHT TO EXTENDED LIFER #1: Burial is murder! Burial is murder! Burial is murder!

RIGHT TO EXTENDED LIFER #2: Save the undead! Save the undead! Save the undead!

[*Lights down on the funeral.*]

NARRATOR: Despite their innocent-looking symbol, the movement stressed confrontation. Funeral homes were fire-bombed. Morticians and embalmers were forced to conceal their identities. Even limo drivers were suspect. Many believed reason would prevail and took comfort in the fact that the movement failed to win mainstream support. However, the ranks of the Anti-Funeralists continued to swell as old members never died off and new recruits were always just a few shovel-fulls away. Inevitably, highly-paid political pollsters were the first to see the writing on the wall.

[*Lights up on a Political Party staff meeting of* POLITICIANS *and their* POLLSTER.]

POLITICIAN #1: Speaking for my constituents, I say cut the heart out of that damned baby and you kill the movement, it's that simple!

POLLSTER: You're dead wrong. Give them what they want. Embrace these people now and they might remember you in the fall.

POLITICIAN #2: But that's insane. We'd be giving the right to vote to the dead!

POLLSTER: Dead, alive—c'mon, this is America—what's the difference?

[*Lights down on the political meeting.*]

NARRATOR: And so, in an historic Rose Garden ceremony, President Lance Ito signed the so-called, "Last Wish Baby Bill" into law. The bill not only granted the living-impaired the right to vote but also guaranteed entitlements and protections historically denied to members of this community, a community long regarded by many narrow-minded Americans as sloven, listless, and euphemistically-speaking, somewhat aromatic. [*Beat.*]

As the years passed and the American political spectrum calcified, living-impaired voters inevitably sought a candidate from among their own ranks. Republican strategists boldly exhumed a former California vote getter whose appeal cut across party lines and living tissue.

[SLIDE *graphic of a corpse-ish looking Ronald Reagan, still sporting a full head of hair.*]

During his first news conference as President, the newly re-elected Ronald Reagan announced his plan to fund and build a massive protective shield which he claimed would act as a deterrent to foreign aggression and help staunch the flow of illegal immigration.

[SLIDE *graphic of the North-American hemisphere as seen from space. Covering the entire continental United States is a huge Egyptian-style pyramid.*]

When completed, the shield did more than defend American shores, it stood as a symbol to all that here was a nation entombed, whose people sought no light to guide them and silenced any sound which might stir them. [*Beat.*] Except one...

[*We hear the growing sound of the thump-thump-thumping of the baby heart as the* SLIDE *of The Last Wish Baby is projected.*]

The never-ceasing, ever-pumping, always-thumping heart of the Original Last Wish Baby.

[*The thumping heart continues as lights slowly fade to black.*]

END OF PLAY

Paul Selig

THE MYSTERY SCHOOL

PAUL SELIG

Paul Selig has had work for the stage produced throughout the U.S. and the United Kingdom. *Three Visitations*, his trilogy of chamber operas with composer Kim D. Sherman, premieres this summer at The New Music-Theatre Ensemble in Minneapolis. His solo work The *Mystery School* will be produced in New York next season by En Gard Arts. Other plays include *Body Parts, Moon City, Terminal Bar* (published *Best Short Plays of 1988-89, Gay Plays 3*), *The Pompeii Traveling Show* (New York Drama League Award), and *Never Enough* (with Shapiro and Smith Dance Co.). He currently serves on the faculty of the NYU Tisch School of the Arts Dramatic Writing Program and Goddard College's M.F.A. in Writing Program. He is a graduate of the Yale School of Drama.

TONGUES

SETTING: *A woman in a church pew. Pantsuit, scarf, heavy make-up, cheap gold jewelry. The sound of a revival meeting in progress fades as she turns to face the audience.*

WOMAN: I am beginning to suspect that some people think that the gift of tongues is given out as freely as rejections to the Four Oaks Country Club. Eunice Blakey, she don't get tongues. She's fakin' it. Last week I was walkin' home from the motel an' I passed by her garage, an' there she was, waxin' her Pinto an' practicin' for Sunday. She's the first one struck down every service. First one passed out in the aisles with her dress up over her head an' her panties wavin' in the face of that cute new usher from Arkansas. First one to confess about pluggin' the milkman when her husband's away, first one to get redeemed every damn week, and don't you just know that it's to let old Arkansas know she's still available for another fall. Last week I got so fed up that as soon as her eyes started rollin' back in her head I jumped outa my pew an' started screamin,' "FAKER! FAKER! THE HOLY SPIRIT DON'T EVEN *KNOW* YOU!"

That shut her up.

She was waitin' for me, sure enough, in the parkin' lot after, like she meant some kinda trouble, an' she said "I do too get the gift of tongues." An' I said, "Yeah, every damn night over at the Motel 6 in every orifice you got. I get to clean up after your messes, case you didn't know, so you best watch your ass with me."

And she said, "Well, my Lord forgives me seventy times upon seventy."

An' I said, "Well, I been counting the condoms in your wastebasket for the past three years an' you done HIT that mark some time ago. Even Jesus got his limits. You best get your privates fireproofed, Eunice, 'cause where you're goin' you're gonna need another kinda protection."

An' she said, "My God is a God of forgiveness."

An' I said, "Not my Lord. Not my Lord."

How dare she pretend to know the Language of the End

Times? And Mary Alice Johnson over there? Her son left the fold to be a tap dancer in Las Vegas. He'd send back pictures of his self with Lola Falana and Debbie Reynolds, and I will tell you which one looked like they had more paint on their faces. She buried him last year. Now she's over at the hospital every week spoonin' out her home baked goods to others like him. Who's just gonna be damned anyway. I don't know what she's thinkin. Might as well send 'em to hell on a full stomach. Burn with powdered sugar on their lips...

I was over there one day when my nephew got his hand caught in the disposal, an' I saw her comin' outa the Sin Ward with all her Tupperware.

An' I said, "Mary Alice, don't you come too close. Who do you think you're foolin'? You know why nobody never buys your damn fool pies at the bake sale? We know where your POTS have been. Don't you just think you're bein' NOBLE?"

An' you know what she had the nerve to tell me?

She said, "I thought I was bein' Christian..."

You'll burn in hell with the rest of them. See if I care. You can go bake for the pansies in the ninth circle of hell. Put your Betty Crocker over a flame down there an' see how fast your dough rises, Miss Mary Alice...

You know what's comin'. You know what's comin'. An' won't it be fine...

Let your cakes rise, Mary Alice, for I too will be rising...

Trudy Wilson what holds the Avon parties had us all in, an' I told her the first trumpet was gettin' ready to blow, an' I wanted to look my best for it, an' to give me the works...

An' she told me not to hold my breath because the trumpets and the breakin' of the seals was all symbolic. She'd seen it on "60 Minutes" where some China man was tellin' about the seven seals bein' the same as the seven centers in the body used for stickin' needles in acupuncture.

She said, "It ain't somethin' from the OUTSIDE that's comin, it's comin from the INSIDE."

An' I told her that if she was listenin' to some Bhuddist crap I would buy my face paint somewhere else. Dina Parks got a Mary Kaye outlet outa her guest room, an' SHE'S been SAVED

An' Trudy says "The scriptures say Our Father, not Our Father if you happen to agree with me."

An' I thought, you pitiful fool, you pitiful fool...

An' Sheila? She's callin' her Psychic Friend from work so many times they decided to dock her pay an' put a block on the 900 numbers.

I said, "What did your psychic friend tell you?" An' she said she got told it was gonna be a big year for her, an' I thought, yeah, well, burnin' in hell for an eternity ain't exactly a little event, an' that's where you're gonna go for listenin' to false prophets...

Every Friday at Bingo, each time somebody wins big, I think, take your money, take your money, you ain't gonna even have time to enjoy it.

All them people here. All them people who's goin' off smilin' an shakin' hands at the end of every service. Them people what's chaperoning the youth groups and sending money to the starvin' children every month and standin' in line like hucksters to ladle out soup for the homeless, who do they think they kiddin'? Who do they think is payin' attention to their works?

"It makes me feel so GOOD," they testify. "It makes me feel so GOOD to be of service."

An' I think, then, come over to MY house an' scrub MY floors, an' come over to the motel with ME an' YOU change the filth on the sheets an' YOU scrub out the toilets an' YOU peel the spunk off the walls that got shot there the night before by your husbands, your good neighbors and your children ...

You come and take this life that has been defiled and YOU fix it right. I'll take your money. I'll go over to the photo booth at the five and ten and send you pictures of ME smiling and write you all a letter every six months tellin' you what I RE-ALLY think of you. It would be my damned pleasure...

You ain't saved. You will no more enter in my Father's house than I will be allowed entrance into your country club. You don't even know the language. And when it comes, you don't even understand...

The right way is narrow. Narrow is the path. I walk into this temple of Pharisees and I know that I am the only one that's leaving. I am the only one here that will not suffer the years of trepidation to come.

Politicians gonna get it. Take my money, give my jobs to wetbacks. Take the prayer outta the schools and teachin' them kids they was mutated outa fungus. I know who's image I am created in.

I tole my brother Larry, "You keep your guns out, Larry. You keep your rifles cleaned, because you ain't gonna be allowed where I'm a goin', an' you're gonna be left here when the locusts come and the Angels of Philadelphia and Smyrna break open their seals of pain upon this world. I will be long gone, but you keep your guns clean so you can shoot to kill. You watch who comes knockin' on your door on the dark night. You watch."

The darkness is real. Each time I kneel in prayer, I see my words moving into it. And it becomes stronger and stronger, and it is a force to be reckoned with. And each time I pray for the end, I see it getin' bigger an' stronger an' more an' more ready to come. More and more ready to topple the cities and smite the unfaithful and bring the glory of the kingdom through the wrath of my God.

Do they all think that He's sittin' up there on His cloud playin Parcheesi with His only begotten Son? Don't you think that the two of them got their maps spread out across the backs of the martyrs and they're stickin' their own black pins in an' plannin out what will be next? Don't you think that they have waited for this time and are GLAD?

Don't you think it's not comin'. It's comin' faster than a Cuban refugee can paddle. In the twinkling of an eye. Swifter than the rain and bigger than a nation and louder than a bomb blast.

For I KNOW the language of the end. It comes to ME. It speaks through ME. [*Body tremor.*] And the governments will tumble, for they are not in truth [*Body tremor.*]...And the mighty will perish, for they are not in truth [*Body tremor, almost speaking in tongues.*]...

It's a comin' it's a comin' it's a comin' it's a comin'.

It's a comin' it's a comin' it's a comin' it's a comin'.

And the years of waiting. All the years of prayin' without an answer will be because of this. When the fires come and the path is too narrow for any of you to follow, when I have been lifted out of my pew and through the roof of this temple, and when I am rising in the clouds and I am lookin' down upon the pitiable masses who have denied my Lord, who have given themselves over to the ways of sin, when my pantyhose is makin' runs in themselves because I am risin' so high and fine above you, and I look at your country clubs burn and I see your building's tumble, and your children, poor things, run screamin' on fire from the school house, while my hair turns into angel hair and my gold necklace melts and rises to become a halo around my head, I will be vindicated and my words will be finally understood...

[*Her body begins to shake wildly as she breaks out into tongues. She rises in her pew, triumphantly, gloriously, for all her congregation to see and hear.*]

AMELIA'S SECOND STEP

SETTING: AMELIA *sits smoking on a folding chair before a shade bearing the twelve steps of A.A. She is in her fifties, has a gray pageboy haircut, and wears a sweatshirt that reads "Serenity Sucks." Her hand is raised defiantly in the air as she glowers at the floor. She responds, as if called on.*

AMELIA: My name is Amelia and you *know* what I am.

First, I would like to make an amends to the group. It was I who put the dead cat in the collection basket during last Thursday's Promises Meeting.

It was an anniversary gift for my former partner, Ingrid, who, as you may know, has since resigned her post as treasurer of this group and has moved on in search of bigger livers to fry over at the Salvation Army Meeting on 14th Street.

Thank you for calling on me, Billy T. I was quite struck by your saying that maybe God gave us all two arms to reach for Him. It was almost as startling as Heidi M's triumph last week when she described herself as a little sober daisy cross pollinating the drunken fields of humanity.

Now, I know what step we're on today, which is why I have taken this opportunity to raise my little pink nailed hand for the

first and LAST time in NINE DRY MONTHS to ask you all
a question that has been burning itself into my detoxifying skull
ever since I first got shanghaied into this rat cellar of Our Lady
Of Perpetual Thirst Church.

HOW DO YOU DO IT?

HOW DO YOU MANAGE TO DO IT?

YOU PEOPLE ALL SPEAK OF COMING TO BE-
LIEVE IN SOME HIGHER POWER AS IF IT WERE AS
NATURAL AS A BODILY FUNCTION.

Ingrid FARTS and she calls it a spiritual awakening!

Ingrid! The love of my life and the bane of my existence,
with whom I shared for fourteen years a room the size of a
colostomy bag on Greenwich Avenue. And it was some kinda
marriage and some kinda honeymoon. You coulda tied the
beercans to our butts and sent us rattling down Seventh, if you
could ever get us out the door.

"Did you take out the garbage?"

"Last week."

"Did you feed the cats?"

"Last week."

And so we lived in alcoholic bliss, surrounded by the mul-
tiple corpses of dead felines and enough trash to start a landfill
in New Jersey.

And I honestly thought we were happy.

And then one day she shows up in the hole in the wall we
called home and she has purchased a vacuum cleaner, with what
should have been our beer money for the month. And she picks
up the remains of Fluffy and Hiowatha and plops them into a
Hefty Bag, and continues to ravage through the debris of our
lives until she gets to me. And she gets to me, and she says,
"Things are gonna change, Amelia. Things are gonna change,
Amelia. Things are gonna change."

And, like a dutiful fool, I follow her here into folding chair
hell, and we count our days in tandem, and we snigger at the
personal revelations that are shared daily with the uniformity of
a Geraldo broadcast. And I do the crosswords in the back, and
Ingrid pretends to listen, and we keep each other away from the
Schlitz and the barroom, and I thought we were still pretty
tight, but something musta got by me.

Because one day old Ingrid comes home and announces that she's found God.

"I've GOT it," she says.

And I said, "Is it CONTAGIOUS?"

And Ingrid the Marxist, and one of the five most intelligent women I have ever known in my life, is standing there before me in her LEDERHOSEN telling me she has seen the proverbial Light.

"Where is it?" I said. "Underneath that stack of *Life Magazines* in the hallway? Behind that fermenting catbox in the kitchen? Did the TOOTH FAIRY come and SLAM it under your dentures while you were sleeping?"

I would like to believe in fairies, Ingrid. I would LIKE to believe in angels. I would LIKE to believe that Shirley McClaine did not accidentally high kick herself in the head during rehearsals for *Can Can* but is actually saying something of possible relevance."

And six months later, prayin' Ingrid's packing her rucksack to follow this light which, for some reason I cannot fathom, has told her to detach herself from toxic, co-dependent, farting old ME, who, unlike her, CANNOT SEEM TO KEEP HERSELF OFF THE SAUCE FOR MORE THAN THREE DAYS, NO MATTER HOW HARD SHE TRIES!!!

WHERE??? WHERE DO I LOOK, INGRID? AFTER YOU? YOUR FUTURE'S WRITTEN ON THE WALLS. SIX MONTHS FROM NOW YOU'RE GONNA BE STANDING IN FRONT OF THE SALVATION ARMY WITH YOUR LIPS WRAPPED AROUND A TUBA NOZZLE LIKE SOME REJECT FROM THE DAUGHTER'S OF BILITIS PRODUCTION OF GUYS AND DOLLS!!!

[*Bringing attention back into room, attempting to regain composure.*]

I heard you say while you were speaking that you didn't believe in coincidence anymore. That, perhaps, coincidence was your Higher Power's way of remaining anonymous. I found that very interesting. I will have to put that in my little sober thinking cap and let it ferment. But, I had a coincidence today. I ran into Ingrid.

Well, it was actually planned, as I had been up all night having a heated debate with an unopened bottle of scotch, which was making an irrefutable argument as to why I shouldn't just drink up, get it over with, and die. And in an absolute panic, I find myself tearing at the *Life Magazines*, and lifting up the catbox, and running, running outa the apartment like a dry drunk outa hell.

And I am waiting, breathless, when Ingrid comes twelve stepping her way down the stairs of the morning meeting.

And I say, "Ingrid, I am not going to make it, and I don't understand..."

And she looks at me in all seriousness, and she starts talking about monkeys...

It seems there are these monkeys, see, on these little boney islands that polka dot the South Seas, and they are starving. And one day, these scientists go and dump all these sweet potatoes in the water, and they gather on the beach of this first island to receive the miracle of the yams.

Now, a YAM is not native cuisine to these creatures. In fact, they had never seen one before. But these little simians, out of sheer hunger and desperation, begin to go through the painful process of learning how to peel and eat a YAM. And first one does it, and then another. And when the hundreth monkey on this one little rock chip finally triumphs and heaves the thing into his gullet, all at once, all the other monkeys on all the neighboring islands, without having to GO through the abject PAIN and HUMILIATION of trial and error, without HAVING to slam their yams against their foreheads in frustration, without SCREECHING to the bloody SKIES that the FOOD which has FINALLY been offered them is inedible, suddenly and miraculously begin to eat them, too.

For, Ingrid is telling me, the new information had been picked up by the race mind. That the species had been permanently altered and filled, but that others had to go before them.

And that it didn't matter to her what I chose to believe in, so long as it was tough enough to keep me from killing myself one fucking day at a time.

And as she is walking away, Ingrid, the Diane Fossey of the A.A. Congo, turns and says: "For all you know, Amelia, you may be the hundredth monkey, and when you come to believe, what might happen then will be too beautiful for words..."

AM I TO TRUST THAT WHILE MY WHOLE LIFE

BLING THROUGH THE AIR LIKE A FLYING
AZOV BROTHER, I HAVE ONLY TO REACH
FOR THIS THING YOU SAY AND SOMEHOW TRUST
THAT I WILL BE CAUGHT?

Because I fear things. I fear change, and I fear that there may indeed be some kind of peace to be found which eludes me. That I have encumbered myself with too many farting belief systems which preclude the simple state of willingness that you describe as the only prerequisite for faith. That I have maligned a truth in ignorance because I am constitutionally incapable of grasping the simplicity behind it. And that you people, who are kind to me no matter what I say and do, really have found some way.

Don't you think I would LIKE to believe in something? Don't you think I would LIKE to believe that the Red Sea did split in two like a dropped cheesecake? Or that a Bhuddha DID find enlightenment under a bodhi tree, or that some messiah did trod the earth two thousand years ago and still does in the hearts of those who've embraced him? Don't you think that even after crawling past the world's religions on my distended belly, I would still like to believe that this thing you've found can fill me, too?

And despite the fact that this action defies all rationality, despite the fact that it poses a terrific threat to all I have ever trusted and held dear, and despite the fact that it may be what is needed to save this cranky old life...

My arms, as if of their own volition...

They are reaching.

[*Lights dim on* AMELIA, *her expression is sad, yet hopeful.*]

DR. EDIE GIVES A COMMENCEMENT SPEECH

SETTING: DR. EDIE, *a happily disheveled woman in her fifties, tries takes her place at a podium festooned with flowers. She wears a ratty fur coat and a corsage. She looks out at her audience with what can only be described as love.*

DR. EDIE: I have been told that today is a special occasion, so I have worn my rat.

All occasions are special to Dr. Edie Kelvin, but I am especially honored because I have been told that I am here to address a room full of people who hear voices.

I have not felt moved to don the skins of a dead animal since the last time I took on a room, which was last Thursday, when I was escorted bodily from a meeting of the American Psychiatric Association, of which I am not a member, on the use of prescription drugs in medicating those suffering from auditory hallucinations.

There, I was heard to scream loudly, "JOAN OF ARC WOULDA BEEN ON PROZAK, MILTON WOULDA BEEN ON THORAZINE, AND *YOU* COCKSUCKERS WOULD HAVE TAKEN THE CANDLES AWAY FROM DICKENSON SO'S SHE COULDN'T BURN AT ALL."

I myself was born hearing voices. And I consider it to be quite a privilege to be invited to share my story with you, who not only hear them, but have the courage to follow what they say.

One winter, many years ago, when Dr. Edie was but a mite, her voices guided her to the bus stop outside the Yeshiva to lie in wait for her current beau, Morty Shine, the sexiest nine year old in Bensonhurst.

When Morty arrived, as the voices promised he would, little Edie was horrified. For Morty appeared before her for the very first time wearing glasses. Thick, ugly, bottle-busters with horned rims that lifted the pais from the sides of his head so's he looked like the Hassidic Pippi Longstocking.

Edie surveyed her ruined boyfriend, and a strange question began to form in her mind. "Morty?" she said. "How did you know you NEEDED them?"

And Morty reported the following:

He hadn't known he needed them. It wasn't until the Festival of Lights, when he had reached to ignite the candles and instead sent his sister up in flames, that his parents wondered if there might not actually be something physically wrong. Because little Shula Shine, though spindly in frame, did not in the least bit resemble their menorah.

Morty Shine, it was revealed, was nearly blind. He had been

his whole life. He had actually managed to survive for nine years on a planet firmly believing that there were nothing but shadows beyond him. And what shocked Edie even more was that up until that day, he had honestly thought that everyone else in the world saw that way, too.

To say that this bit of information confused little Edie would be an understatement. For she had never before conceived of the notion of a "subjective" reality. She had assumed, like Morty, that everyone else thought exactly as she did. And she began to mistrust herself, worrying that perhaps she, too, was wrong, and deceived by what she saw ... and heard ... around her.

And, as if enraged by her refusal to bear witness to her truth, the voices that had always accompanied her through her days began to turn ...

And became cruel.

As Dr. Edie aged, they got louder. Harsh and horrible. They spoke of Dr. Edie's mistakes. Her failed marriage. Her unfinished dissertation. The child miscarried one night after an evening of ballroom dancing with a husband who was no longer hers. The voices told her that she was not enough, and Dr. Edie, frightened and alone, agreed.

In those days, Gawd spoke to her in different ways than he does now. He spoke to her in instances, unable to be heard through the clamor and din inside Dr. Edie's unprescribed head.

And the instances began to lead her, slowly, as she pulled herself through the thickness of days and the darkness of nights to a hotel room on West 72nd Street. Where the transients lived. Other women without settlements. Those whose voices had been silenced, by themselves, and by a world that no longer believes that simply being a human being is cause enough for respect.

For some people are born with less skin than others. Some people are born with almost none at all. They bleed through their clothing as they walk down the street, and their eyes shine brightly in the anticipation of being struck.

Gawd spoke to Dr. Edie in instances then. Through signs. Through symbols. Through the changing of a streetlight that might lead her down an alley, that might lead her to a stranger who might smile in passing, with a kindness in the eyes ...

And then one day, when she was lookin' to get in outa the

rain, she found herself standing in the doorway of Teachers College. And Gawd spoke to her directly, saying "Enter, Edie Kelvin, for I have made you for this love..."

"You made me for what?" I said. "Gawd, you made me for this love?" And I said to him "What is in it for me? Because being a cheerleader ain't my idea of success, and being kind ain't my idea of strength, and teaching the young five days a week ain't my idea of a high time, so's ya know."

Well, Gawd come back to me an' he said, "Edie, you have been created for this because you got the passion to prove me right. You got the knowledge of the night scares to make it better for them in the day, and they will recognize it. They will know it in your smile and see it in your eyes that the pain of being can be mellowed into compassion."

And I screamed, "Gawd, you got the wrong chickie here. You got the wrong bird."

And he said, "Who are you to tell me such things? You will do fine."

And so he sent me to Herbert Lehman High School in the Bronx, where the chairs in the faculty lounge ain't been upholstered since the WPA, and the water fountain sends up blisters for fluid.

He sent me to Herbert Lehman High School, where the students are black, and much to Dr. Edie's horror, all looked alike.

At first.

And then one day from her chalkboard she looked out across the sea of hope, and she began to notice how many shades of brown there were before her, and how much light was in the eyes of those she addressed, and how their potential radiated from them, like a flame threatening to devour her.

And she was humbled by this. She was humbled by their potential, and she was deeply ashamed at what she had done with her own. She had cried herself to sleep too many nights with what might have been, and there she was now, confronted with the possibilities of what could be, might be, with a little bit of encouragement.

And she began to teach to their potential as if it was the most holy thing ever created. Because in Dr. Edie's mind it was holy. And she saw in each of them the tree that might grow from the seed, and she never once let that vision slip from her mind. And every day her innocence was reborn. Every day, she saw the potential in them, the beauty that was created in them come forth, she was reminded of her own.

Because for all she had been through, and for all the wrinkles on her skin, she was not so different.

And suddenly, the flame that had lain dormant and hidden inside her own bosom began to burn, and the voices that had always been there, censoring her, demanding her silence, one by one, began to sing...

"WEND YOUR WAY, BABIES," I say now, and I watch them stumble forward into their lives, and they are so very brave. They have such expectation on their faces. They have such hope in their hearts.

And I SEE myself standing onna mountain screaming out, "WEND YOUR WAY, BABIES." And I wave, and I clap, and I applaud for 'em all, because they are righteous in their being, and they are noble in their efforts, and they are loved, LOVED by Dr. Edie Kelvin. Because they are making their way back into the forest and she knows what lays ahead. And, still they go. Still they go because they are young, and because they must. And perhaps when the nights are dark and cold, and the brambles on the path try to tear at their precious skins, they will remember old Edie, and what she said, and that someone once looked at them with the kindness in their eyes. And if they choose to, they have each other, and that is a fine and righteous thing.

SO WEND YOUR WAY, BABIES. WEND YOUR WAY. And you're gonna cry sometimes, but that's part of it. Because this is a Big School and you grade yourself, so you might as well be generous in your assessment. And if you don't do it, somebody else is gonna do it for you, and they might not be. Because in the long run, babies, what does it matter? What does it matter what they think and what they say? What does it matter what they do to ya? 'Cause you got yourself two feet made by Gawd, and you keep asking THEM to take you to the next fight place, and there you gonna be, babies. There you gonna be.

And if Dr. Edie could, she would walk before you. And she would bat away the terrors with the umbrella she carries with her always. She would beat away the monsters on the trail and she would make sweet beds of moss and leaves for her babies to lie in when they are tired.

But, then she would not be a good teacher. Then, she would not be wise and honor all the wisdom that she sees in her young.

So she prays at night for them. Loudly. And she celebrates them. Each and every mistake that is made along the way she applauds as loudly as the victories, because Dr. Edie KNOWS how learning occurs. And she says, "Lord, make their paths WIDE. No narrow paths for MY young. Make their paths WIDE, and let them know all there is to know. And let them suffer, and rejoice and grow wild in their own ways. But let them stay gentle. For gentleness is not weakness. It's an act of cowardice to be cruel, because you never gotta see the repercussions. People tend to cry in private, and by then you have turned away...

And those nights, when they come home from the jobs they said they'd never take, and they lay on their beds and think they are not enough, Dr. Edie will travel to them, travel through time and space with her rat flying and her umbrella beatin' at the wind, and say, "Oh, yes you are. Oh, yes you are."

And you practice your tuba on the subway. And you finish your novel in the attic room when the kids have gone to bed and the husband's had his fill. And you paint your pictures in grease on the skillet of the fast food if you have to, but then invite all the customers in to see.

And you tell your stories on the street corner, and at the tables in your twelve step meetings, and to the cop who gives you the ticket, and to the doctor who threatens to put you away. But you are never silent.

And you pray at night for the courage to continue expressing your truth, and know that Gawd always answers a prayer like that. And know that your truth may change, as Dr. Edie's has, before she remembered who she was. Because Dr. Edie divorced herself many years ago, and has paid alimony for it ever since. But she is NOT PAYING ANYMORE. And she will NOT BE SILENCED.

And she will continue shouting her truth, until the men in white come and carry her off screaming and hollering, and she will wear her rat proudly from this day forth. For hers is a Holy

War, and she will always honor the voices that tell her where to turn...

And if you would accuse Dr. Edie Kelvin of being an idealist, just think for a moment, and know that you are the kind of person who believes that having an ideal is something to be accused of.

Because in the final analysis, babies, it's your own voices you gotta follow. Not old Dr. Edie's. She hears her own...

Let yours be kind ones.

CURTAIN

Mac Wellman

THE SANDALWOOD BOX

The Sandalwood Box was originally commissioned and produced by the McCarter Theate, Princeton, NJ.

MAC WELLMAN

Poet and playwright Mac Wellman was born in Cleveland and is a resident of New York City. Recent productions include: *Tallahassee* (Len Jenkin) at the Workhouse Theater; *Swoop* and *Dracula* at Soho Rep; *The Hyacinth Macaw* and *A Murder of Crows* (at Primary Stages and elsewhere); and *The Land of Fog and Whistles* (as part of the Whitney /Philip Morris "Performance on 42nd Street" series). He has received numerous honors, including both National Endowment for the Arts and John Simon Guggenheim Fellowships. In 1990, he received a *Village Voice* Obie (Best New American Play) for *Bad Penny, Terminal Hip* and *Crowbar*. In 1991, he received another Obie for *Sincerity Forever*. Two collections of his plays have recently been published: *The Bad Infinity* (PAJ/Johns Hopkins University Press) and *Two Plays* (Sun & Moon). Sun & Moon also published *A Shelf In Woop's Clothing*, his third collection of poetry, and two novels: *The Fortuneteller* (1991), and *Annie Salem* (1996).

The Maiden caught me in the Wild
Where I was dancing merrily
She put me into her cabinet
And locked me up with a golden key
from "The Crystal Cabinet"

       by William Blake

CHARACTERS

MARSHA GATES   A student and prop-girl at Great Wind Repertory Theater.

PROFESSOR CLAUDIA MITCHELL   A Professor of Cataclysm at Great Wind University.

BUS DRIVER

CHORUS OF VOICES   including: DOCTOR GLADYS STONE; OSVALDO (A sadistic monster); and others from the House of the Unseen.

Note: The occasional appearance of an asterisk in the middles of a speech indicates that the next speech begins to overlap at that point. A double asterisk indicates that a later speech (not the one immediately following) begins to overlap at that point. The overlapping speeches are all clearly marked in the text.

SETTING: *In the rain forest of South Brooklyn.*

SCENE 1

We see MARSHA, *alone. Except for the table and the sandalwood box itself, all scenic devising is done vocally. The actor speaking her* VOICEOVER (VO) *appears in a pool of light down right; she bears a strong resemblance to* DOCTOR CLAUDIA MITCHELL.

MARSHA (VO): My name is Marsha Gates. I lost my voice on the 9th of November, 1993, as a result of an act of the Unseen. If you think you cannot be so stricken, dream on.

CHORUS: I took the IRT every other day for speech therapy. In a remote part of Brooklyn. Avenue X. Where my therapist, an angelic person, resides. Her name is Gladys Stone.

SINGLE CHORUSTER: Doctor Gladys Stone.

[*The good* DOCTOR *appears.* MARSHA *tries to speak.*]

MARSHA: . . .?(!) . . .

[DOCTOR STONE *tries to speak.*]

DOCTOR STONE: . . .!(?) . . .

MARSHA (VO): Doctor Stone tried to cure me. Alas, she too was stricken.

[*Since neither can speak both give it up. Pause.*]

CHORUS: Dream on I did, but . . .

[*The good* DOCTOR *disappears.*]

MARSHA (VO): Parallel lines meet in Brooklyn. The East and West side IRT. This geometry is also of the Unseen. It is inhuman design, and therefore unnameable. Also, the knowledge of its mystery* is subject to error.

CHORUS: It is human to be so* stricken.

MARSHA GATES: I took the wrong train. We're on the wrong train.

MARSHA (VO): I took the wrong train and arrived at a strange place. A place I did not know. The air felt humid and tropical. The air felt not of the city I knew. A lush, golden vegetation soared up, up and all around the familiar landscape of the city, like a fantastic aviary. It was a fantastic aviary. A place full of exotic specimens. [*Pause.*] It occurred to me I might have lost my mind as well, although I did not think so because the idea gave me such strange pleasure, like the touch of a feather along the top of my hand. This place seemed a paradise. I laughed and fell asleep. I dreamed . . .

CHORUS: I am waiting at a bus stop, waiting to return to my home. Another person is standing there with me. We're at the bus-stop by the Aviary.

PROFESSOR CLAUDIA MITCHELL: Hiya.

MARSHA GATES: Hello.

PROFESSOR CLAUDIA MITCHELL: I'm Professor Claudia Mitchell.

MARSHA GATES: I'm Marsha Gates, a part-time student.

PROFESSOR CLAUDIA MITCHELL: I'm an archeologist, of sorts.

MARSHA GATES: I'm a student at City College. No declared major. I also work part-time in a theater. Great Wind Repertory. The plays are all shit. TV with dirty words.

PROFESSOR CLAUDIA MITCHELL: I see.

MARSHA GATES: I can't speak, either.

PROFESSOR CLAUDIA MITCHELL: So I understand.

MARSHA GATES: It's very aggravating.

PROFESSOR CLAUDIA MITCHELL: So it would seem. [*Pause.*] My specialty is human catastrophe.

MARSHA GATES: That's very nice, but you're making me nervous.

PROFESSOR CLAUDIA MITCHELL: So it would seem.

MARSHA GATES: Is this the Zoological Gardens? The beasts seem to be making a considerable noise. Perhaps the person who is supposed to . . . feed them—

CHORUS: Has been stricken,* like you, by an act of the Unseen.

MARSHA GATES: Like me. And Doctor Gladys Stone.

PROFESSOR CLAUDIA MITCHELL: I see. Perhaps so. Perhaps, however, you mean an act of complete probabilistic caprice. A fly in the Unseen's ointment. An ontological whigmaleery. A whim of the die.

MARSHA GATES: I work in the theater. Philosophy makes me nervous.

PROFESSOR CLAUDIA MITCHELL: I see. What theater?

MARSHA GATES: I am a prop girl at Great Wind Rep. I told you.

[*The* PROFESSOR *throws back her head and laughs. Pause.*]

PROFESSOR CLAUDIA MITCHELL: An artist! Then surely you must appreciate the higher things in life. Knowledge. Ideas pertaining to a theory of the world Id. The power of the mind to crank out ideational constructs beyond mere calculation and desire . . . not to mention . . . mere mortality.

MARSHA GATES: This bus sure is taking a long time.

CHORUS: The bus arrives in a wild rotation of dust, hot fumes and the clangor of the unmuffled internal combustion engine. All are deafened. An instrument of noise close to the heart of disaster.

BUS DRIVER: Ever seen a bus before? This is a bus. Don't just stand there quaking. We in the bus business don't have all day. We live complex lives. We dream, gamble, seek, deserve a better fate than Time or Destiny, through the agency of the Unseen, allows. So, get aboard if you are going to. If you dare. There, there in the valley, someone is playing a saxophone among the peonies. His heart is broke. There's no poop in his pizzle and surely the will of the Unseen shall bear witness, and lift him up from the abyss of his . . . of his wretchedness, to the bright aire above where lizards, snakes and the mythic tortoise are . . . glub, glub . . . My basket of sandwiches flew off into the cheese that is the North end of the thing in the hot ladder. Groans and slavver. Spit and questions marked on the margin. A sale of snaps, larval coruscations. Sweet drug of oblivion. On a global scale. Flowers of unknown radiance, snarls of snails, all of a coral wonder. Just in time for the man who discovers himself stubbed, in an ashtray. Put out. All the work of the Unseen, like a wind in the sail of our hour, midnight, when we encounter the Adversary, anarchic and covered with hairs, in the form of our good neighbor's discarded sofa, left out for the garbage man to pick up. He would like to discover the truth about what can do no harm only if it is kept, safely under lock and key, in its cage, with no poop in its pizzle, aware of us but dimly, us lost in the crunching despair of our endless opening up before the doings of the Unseen, in all our sick, sad, pathetic innocence. Innocence that is only the half-cracked euphemism for our woe, which possesses not even the required token for the train, or bus. Nor even the train to the plane. Not even the faith to enact that pizzle.

MARSHA GATES: I don't have a token.* Do you have a token?

PROFESSOR CLAUDIA MITCHELL: No, I don't have a token. Do you have a token?

[*They look at each other hopelessly. Pause.*]

BUS DRIVER: Then what are you wasting my time for?

PROFESSOR CLAUDIA MITCHELL: And he drove off, leaving us both in a brown study, abandoned. So I turned to my young companion, green with anxiety, and spoke in what I imagined were soothing tones... [*Long pause.*]

PROFESSOR CLAUDIA MITCHELL: [*Cont'd.*] I collect catastrophes. Vitrified catastrophes. Enchanted in a case of glass. Encased in glass,* that is.

MARSHA GATES: What a mess.* Farblonjet.

PROFESSOR CLAUDIA MITCHELL: You like messes?* Aha.

MARSHA GATES: What a* disaster.

PROFESSOR CLAUDIA MITCHELL: So you are fond of* disaster!

MARSHA GATES: What a catastrophe!

PROFESSOR CLAUDIA MITCHELL: Quelle Catastrophe! I collect them, you know.

MARSHA GATES: What did you say?

PROFESSOR CLAUDIA MITCHELL: I collect catastrophes.* Vitrified, of course.

MARSHA GATES: No, the other thing you said.

PROFESSOR CLAUDIA MITCHELL: Vitrified. Encased in glass. They are very beautiful. Would you like to see my collection? My estate is very close, just beyond the lianas.

MARSHA GATES: No, no. The other thing* you said.

PROFESSOR CLAUDIA MITCHELL: Never mind. Never mind. That was in the French language. The language of love.

[*They exchange long, hard looks.*]

CHORUS: So I went to her house. In the deep Forest, near Avenue X. I went with her, although I knew there was something about it not quite right. [*Pause.*] Something, in fact, quite wicked.

MARSHA (VO): I suspected that my hostess, Doctor Claudia Mitchell, harbored heretical views on the topic of the Unseen.

CHORUS: Heh-heh . . . [*Pause.*] . . . heh-heh . . .

[*She looks hard at the* PROFESSOR.]

MARSHA (VO): I could not bring myself to ask. Her draperies were of the finest brocade, purple and stiff, annihilating the out of doors with its pedestrian bird-cries, bus fumes, the horror of the city's . . . hullabaloo . . .

CHORUS: Tick-tock . . . tick-tock . . . [*Repeat, etc.*]

PROFESSOR CLAUDIA MITCHELL: I poured a large glass of sherry for the young girl, and myself, and led her into my studio.

MARSHA (VO): There, upon a long, dark-grained, baroque table of immense, carved teak, supported by four, grotesque, dragon-faced whorls of some other, strange wood, lay . . . tada!

PROFESSOR CLAUDIA MITCHELL: My sandalwood box. Within it, my dear Marsha, is nestled my collection.

MARSHA (VO): The deep plush of the box's dark interior . . . took my breath away.

[*The* CHORUS *joins* MARSHA *and the* PROFESSOR *around the sandalwood box.*]

PROFESSOR CLAUDIA MITCHELL: This is. . . [*She holds up a small, bright object.*] Seoul, Korea. December 25th, 1971. The worst hotel fire in history. An eight-hour blaze at the 222 room Taeyokale Hotel. A total of 163 persons are incinerated or succumb to the horrors of noxious inhalation. Two workmen are later sent to prison for terms of three to five years, convicted of carelessness in the handling of gasoline. [*Pause. She replaces it in its place and holds up another.*] This is Clontarf, Ireland in the year 1014 A.D. Danish raiders under chieftain Sweyn the First (Forkbeard) are repelled by the forces of King Brian Boru. The Danes are mauled, with a loss of 6,000, and driven back to their stumpy ships. Both Boru and his son are killed. Forkbeard is slain later that year. And another. Saint Gotthard Pass, Italian Alps. 1478. During the private war between the Duke of Milan and another feudal lord, an array of 60 stout Zurichers, allies of the Milanese are flattened by an avalanche in the early afternoon, with the solar furnace blazing away so innocently above.* And another. Kossovo, in former Yugoslavia. 1389. Prince Lazar's Serbian army of 25,000 meets

the Spahis and Janazaries of Sultan Murad in the morning mists
of the 28th of June. In accordance with a prophecy of the Unseen, the entire Serbian force is annihilated, thus clearing the
way for Turkish mastery of the region for over half a millennium.
And another. The Johnstown Flood. May 31, 1889. A wall of water 30 to 40 feet high bursts down upon the town as the entire
damn collapses. Over two thousand people are drowned, or
dragged to their deaths over tree branches, barbed wires and
overturned houses. Victims continue to be unearthed, some far
upstream, for the next seventeen years. Yet another. The retreat
of the French Army from Moscow, begun on October 19th,
1812. Hounded cruelly by marauding Russian guerrillas, the
Grande Armee is soon mangled, and beaten—reduced to a desperate, starving horde. Snows begin to fall on November 4. Ten
days later Napoleon is left with only 25,000 able-bodied fighters.
At the River Berezina 10,000 stragglers are abandoned in the
crossing on the 29th. French losses are the worst in history:
400,000 men, 175,000 horses, 1000 cannon. [*Pause.*] This wonderful collection constitutes only a merest part of the world's catastrophe, which in toto comprises the dark side of the Unseen's
id.

MARSHA (VO): But I hardly heard the words she spoke because of a
curious feeling that stole into my mind, and I began to wonder,
out-loud—

MARSHA GATES: Why is the night better than the day? Why do the
young become old, and not the other way around? Why is the
world made mostly of clay? Why can't a person always tell what
is wrong from what is right? Why does the full weight of the
Unseen fall most heavily upon the visible, like brass? Why can't
we see what it is that compels both cause and effect to be so in-
terfixed? Why can't I find a number beyond which nothing can
be enumerated? Why can't I know what will come of what I do,
think, and say? Why can't I know truth from lies the way I do
"up" from "down." Why is one person's disaster not catastrophe
for all? And who knows why these things are called unaccounted.
Unaccountable. Uncountable. And why, oh why, don't we know
who does know the answers to these things? [*Pause.*] ... because
isn't it so that if we possess, and are possessed by a question, the

answer must, too, be hidden somewhere, somewhere in the heart of someone, someone real, and not a phantom of the Unseen?

CHORUS: Dream on, they did. Dream on...

MARSHA (VO): When, however, I perceived at last the true sickness of her id...her sick, squat, demented id...I stepped quietly behind her while she was focused on her precious set of vitrified catastrophes...and picked up a large, blunt object to bludgeon her with, but...

[*Picks up a chair, freezes. The* PROFESSOR *turns to her, freezes. Pause. They look at each other a long time.*]

MARSHA (VO): When I saw she wanted me to do it...she wanted me to do it...out of a curious...covetous...vexatious...perversity...[*Slowly* MARSHA *lowers the chair.*]

PROFESSOR CLAUDIA MITCHELL: I am a recovering alcoholic, and a fraud.

MARSHA GATES: And I knew she was neither...so—

CHORUS: Out of a curious, covetous, vexatious perversity...

MARSHA (VO): [*Very softly.*] I refuse, I refuse, I refuse* to do it...

CHORUS: I REFUSE TO BLUDGEON* HER.

MARSHA GATES: Simply put: I refused to do* it.

CHORUS: She refused.

[*She laughs. The* PROFESSOR *roars out a command.*]

PROFESSOR CLAUDIA MITCHELL: **Osvaldo! Osvaldo!** Throbow hobero obobout.

[*The* CHORUS *beats her up, and throws her out. As this is being done we hear the following, sung by the* PROFESSOR *and* MARSHA (VO).]

PROFESSOR CLAUDIA MITCHELL AND MARSHA GATES (VO):
In the name of Id
And all the Id's work
Show me what dark works
Are done in the dark.
In the name of disaster.
In the name of catastrophe.

[*Pause. She lies outside the door of the* PROFESSOR'S *house, dazed. We hear birds cry.*]

MARSHA (VO): Her man, an ape named "Osvaldo," beat me, and threw me out, but... [*Pause. She opens her hand revealing one small, glimmering object.*]

CHORUS: As I lay, bloody and beaten, on the Forest floor amongst dead leaves and whatnot, nearly poisoned by lethal inhalation of spoors, and accidental ingestion of strange moss and fennel...

PROFESSOR CLAUDIA MITCHELL: Wicked id's fennel...

MARSHA (VO): I opened my hand, and my voice returned. I had stolen one small, nearly perfect catastrophe.

[*A slow blackout begins.*]

MARSHA GATES: April 4, 1933. The United States dirigible Akron goes down in heavy seas, in a remote spot in the middle of the Atlantic Ocean with a loss of 73 nearly perfect lives.

[*Pause.*]

MARSHA (VO): It was the most perfect jewel of that Sandalwood box.

END OF PLAY.

BEST AMERICAN SHORT PLAYS
1992-1993

The Best American Short Play series includes a careful mixture of offerings from many prominent established playwrights, as well as up and coming younger playwrights. These collections of short plays truly celebrates the economy and style of the short play form. Doubtless, a must for any library!

Little Red Riding Hood by **BILLY ARONSON** • Dreamers by **SHEL SILVERSTEIN** •Jolly by **DAVID MAMET** • Show by **VICTOR BUMBALO** • A Couple With a Cat by **TONY CONNOR** • Bondage by **DAVID HENRY HWANG** The Drowning of Manhattan by **JOHN FORD NOONAN** The Tack Room by **RALPH ARZOOMIAN** • The Cowboy, the Indian and the Fervent Feminist by **MURRAY SCHISGAL** • The Sausage Eaters by **STEPHEN STAROSTA** • Night Baseball by **GABRIEL TISSIAN** • It's Our Town, Too by **SUSAN MILLER** • Watermelon Rinds by **REGINA TAYLOR** • Pitching to the Star by **DONALD MARGULIES** • The Valentine Fairy by **ERNEST THOMPSON** • Aryan Birth by **ELIZABETH PAGE**

$15.95 • Paper • ISBN 1-55783-166-1 • $29.95 • Cloth • ISBN 1-55783-167-X

BEST AMERICAN SHORT PLAYS
1991-1992

Making Contact by **PATRICIA BOSWORTH** • Dreams of Home by **MIGDALIA CRUZ** • A Way with Words by **FRANK D. GILROY** • Prelude and Liebestod by **TERRENCE MCNALLY** • Success by **ARTHUR KOPIT** • The Devil and Billy Markham by **SHEL SILVERSTEIN** • The Last Yankee by **ARTHUR MILLER** • Snails by **SUZAN-LORI PARKS** • Extensions by **MURRAY SCHISGAL** • Tone Clusters by **JOYCE CAROL OATES** • You Can't Trust the Male by **RANDY NOOJIN** • Struck Dumb by **JEAN-CLAUDE VAN ITALLIE**

and **JOSEPH CHAIKIN** • The Open Meeting by **A.R.GURNEY**

$12.95 • Paper • ISBN 1-55783-113-0 • $25.95 • Cloth • ISBN 1-55783-112-2

BEST AMERICAN SHORT PLAYS
1990

Salaam, Huey Newton, Salaam by **ED BULLINS** • Naomi in the Living Room by **CHRISTOPHER DURANG** • The Man Who Climbed the Pecan Trees by **HORTON FOOTE** • Teeth by **TINA HOWE** • Sure Thing by **DAVID IVES** • Christmas Eve on Orchard Street by **ALLAN KNEE** • Akhmatova by **ROMULUS LINNEY** • Unprogrammed by **CAROL MACK** • The Cherry Orchard by **RICHARD NELSON** • Hidden in This Picture by **AARON SORKIN** • Boy Meets Girl by **WENDY WASSERSTEIN** • Abstinence by **LANFORD WILSON**

$12.95 • Paper • ISBN 1-55783-085-1 • $23.95 •Cloth • ISBN 1-55783-084-3

BEST AMERICAN SHORT PLAYS
1994–1995

"THE WORK IS FIRST RATE! IT IS EXCITING TO FIND THIS COLLECTION OF TRULY SHORT PLAYS BY TRULY ACCOMPLISHED PLAYWRIGHTS...IDEAL FOR SCHOOL READING AND WORKSHOP PRODUCTIONS..." —KLIATT

A Stye of the Eye by **CHRISTOPHER DURANG** • Buck Simple by **CRAIG FOLS** • Two Mens'es Daughter by **J.e. FRANKLIN** • An Interview by **DAVID MAMET** • WASP by **STEVE MARTIN** • Hot Line by **ELAINE MAY** Life Support by **MAX MITCHELL** • The Whole Shebang by **RICH ORLOFF** • Dear Kenneth Blake by **JACQUELYN REINGOLD** • The Cannibal Masque by **RONALD RIBMAN** • The Artist and the Model by **MURRAY SCHISGAL** • The Spelling of Coynes by **JULES TASCA** • The Wreck on the 5:25 by **THORNTON WILDER** • Lot 13: The Bone Violin by **DOUG WRIGHT**

$15.95 • Paper • ISBN 1-55783-232-3 • $29.95 • Cloth • ISBN 1-55783-231-5

BEST AMERICAN SHORT PLAYS
1993–1994

Window of Opportunity by **JOHN AUGUSTINE** • Barry, Betty, and Bill by **RENÉE TAYLOR/JOSEPH BOLOGNA** • Come Down Burning by **KIA CORTHRON** • For Whom the Southern Belle Tolls by **CHRISTOPHER DURANG** • The Universal Language by **DAVID IVES** • The Midlife Crisis of Dionysus by **GARRISON KEILLOR** • The Magenta Shift by **CAROL MACK** • My Left Breast by **SUSAN MILLER** • The Interview by **JOYCE CAROL OATES** • Tall Tales from The Kentucky Cycle by **ROBERT SCHENKKAN** • Blue Stars by **STUART SPENCER** • An Act of Devotion by **DEBORAH TANNEN** • Zipless by **ERNEST THOMPSON** • Date With a Stranger by **CHERIE VOGELSTEIN**

$15.95 • Paper • ISBN 1-55783-199-8 • $29.95 • Cloth • ISBN 1-55783-200-5